All The Way From Kingdom Come

All The Way From Kingdom Come

Basic Future Events

Philip W. McCarty

Author of *God: A Self Portrait*

iUniverse, Inc.
New York Lincoln Shanghai

All The Way From Kingdom Come
Basic Future Events

Copyright © 2006 by Philip Wayne McCarty

All rights reserved. No part of this book may be used or reproduced by any means, graphic, electronic, or mechanical, including photocopying, recording, taping or by any information storage retrieval system without the written permission of the publisher except in the case of brief quotations embodied in critical articles and reviews.

iUniverse books may be ordered through booksellers or by contacting:

iUniverse
2021 Pine Lake Road, Suite 100
Lincoln, NE 68512
www.iuniverse.com
1-800-Authors (1-800-288-4677)

ISBN-13: 978-0-595-40370-7 (pbk)
ISBN-13: 978-0-595-84745-7 (ebk)
ISBN-10: 0-595-40370-0 (pbk)
ISBN-10: 0-595-84745-5 (ebk)

Printed in the United States of America

Contents

Introduction vii
First Things First 1
Looks Like This Is The End 17
Not In A Thousand Years 29
The Tribulation Players 51
The Tribulation Plot 71
You're Outta Here 95
When It's All Been Said And Done 109
Appendix:
    An Accepter's Story 119

Introduction

The majority of what I see passing for teaching about future events is nothing more than the ventings of conspiracy theorists. If you are picking up this book to try to find out the name of the Anti-Christ, or to know which nations are going to make up his ten-member confederacy, then you need to put this book down now and walk away.

The goal of this book is to provide a person with the basics of what the Bible says is coming in our future. It is intended for people who may not be familiar with the Bible, or with the terminology used when people speak about future events. In other words, if you don't know what the words "Anti-Christ" or "ten-member confederacy" refer to, then this book is for you.

I have tried to write this book so it is understandable to everyone, no matter what your level of prior knowledge is on the subject. But, please remember that a writer should know his topic well. Because of this, there are times when a writer will forget his audience does not know something, and will plow ahead as if they do. I have tried to avoid this, but I think it is inevitable that this will happen somewhere along the way.

Now, you don't know me, so there is going to be a trust issue going on as you begin this book. Whenever you pick up a book written by someone you are not familiar with, there should be some hesitation on your part to immediately trust that what they are saying is right. I have tried to acknowledge this fact and arrange the book in such a way that we will be able to build that trust as we go along. There are some controversial topics to be dealt with in the study of future events. But, there are also some areas where there is a lot of agreement.

In arranging this book it was decided to begin with an area where there is agreement by almost everyone and then proceed into the more controversial subjects. It is hoped that the trust will have been firmly established by the time we reach the most controversial topic. Therefore, we will start our study together by looking at where people will spend eternity. The next step will be to look at the millennial kingdom of Jesus, which is somewhat controversial. We will really be proceeding backwards from the way most writers approach the subject of future events. Most authors begin with the topic of the rapture, but, because it is the most controversial, it will be our last stop.

You will not find me making many assumptions. I have a Bachelor of Arts degree in Bible from Tennessee Temple University, so I like to stick with what the scripture says. If I do stray into the area of my opinion, I will let you know. I will use words like "I think" or "I believe." But, for the most part, this will be a study in what the scripture says. It will not be a study in current events, or assumption.

This book has been nearly twenty years in the making. It is my hope that the material is relevant, and easily understood. It is my prayer that you will gain in your knowledge and understanding of the holy and loving God.

First Things First

> **READ:** REVELATION 4 & 5

It would be unwise to just jump right into the study of future events without first getting some context in which to place the events, or without preparing our minds and hearts so we can better understand the purpose of God revealing future events to us. God prepared the Apostle John to receive and understand the vision of future events he was about to see and record in Revelation. We will look at how God prepared John, then we will see the purpose for us to study future events, and finally we will look at some cautions we must observe when dealing with Bible prophecy.

The Apostle John, one of Jesus' close disciples, wrote the book of Revelation while he was exiled on the Isle of Patmos. John was there because he was a prisoner of the Roman government. His crime was preaching Jesus as the Savior. But God took this time to show the disciple He loved what would take place for the world in the future.

The book begins with Jesus giving John a message to seven churches in Asia Minor. These were real churches, and most of the messages were a mixture of praise and condemnation. We can see the characteristics of these first century churches in churches today.

When Jesus was finished presenting His message to the churches, He did not just begin showing John visions of the future. Instead, John is called into the throne room of God in heaven. This throne room is mission control for the coming events John will see spread out before him. God reveals Himself to John. The attributes, or characteristics, of God that John sees here are the basis for the coming events on the earth.

We are not going to spend time trying to unravel the symbolism of everything John records as being in the throne room. That would be a book in itself. What John records, he actually saw. He was trying to describe things no one had ever seen before. In order to give the reader some idea as to what he was looking at, he used the words "like" and "as" often. He tried to relate what he saw to things we could identify with here on earth. This does not mean that John was simply writing in symbolic language. There really was a physical throne, with beasts surrounding it. There was a physical sea like crystal, and twenty-four elders sitting around the throne. If we get caught up in the surroundings, we will miss the true focus of the scene John records.

Revelation chapter four focuses on God the Father, the One on the throne. It is a scene of worship as the four beasts cry out, "Holy, holy, holy, Lord God Almighty, which was, and is, and is to come." The twenty-four elders cast their crowns before the throne in worship and declare the One on the throne worthy "to receive glory and honor and power." This is the most awesome, continuous worship service there is, and through John we get a glimpse of it.

But, why would God bring John to this scene first? Why bother showing John the throne room of heaven? Because, without a proper perspective of God, John will not understand all that he is about to be shown. The cry of the beasts gives us important information about God's character. Three times they cry out that God is holy. Holiness is the root of God. Yes, we know God is love, but God always seems to emphasize His holiness. Isaiah was immediately struck with the holiness of God, when God revealed Himself to him (Isaiah 6:1–7). At the burning bush, Moses was told to take off his shoes because he was standing on holy ground (Exodus 3:1–10). God even commanded us to be holy because He is holy (Leviticus 11:45). Apparently God would rather we remember that He is holy, than that He is love.

A good definition of holiness is, "embracing what is right to the exclusion of what is wrong." God's very nature is absolute goodness, or holiness. It is the core of His being. For God to ever do, or think, anything bad or evil would destroy His being, His presence.

Think of it this way. Each one of us has a dark side that we want to hide from other people. Admit it. When you go on a date, or a job interview, or meet the neighbors, there are parts of your life and character that you would rather they not find out about. It is that part of us that, when it presents itself, creates negative consequences for us or someone else. The word the Bible uses to identify this dark side is sin.

God does not have this dark side. He does nothing that ultimately creates a negative consequence for Him or others. He is full of absolute goodness. But, because the dark side exists in us, we are in conflict with God. It is the classic good versus evil. God tries everything He can to get us to make good decisions and do good actions, while we try to hide our dark side and sometimes refuse to do what is good.

It is because of this conflict that we sometimes see God as being angry and harsh. We think He is creating negative consequences by punishing people. In fact, God is simply trying to get our attention to do what is right. Punishments go to those who have done something wrong. They have chosen a dark destructive path, and God wants them to get off that path and move toward a good path. The holiness of God will fight against evil for the greater good of all.

The four creatures also declare God to be the Lord God Almighty. God is Lord, which means He is sovereign and has the right to rule everything in heaven and earth. He is the One Who will control the events John will soon see. He is also the Almighty, which means He is all powerful. God has the power to uphold His sovereignty and holiness. He is capable of protecting His right to rule, and keeping Himself pure and holy.

The four creatures also declared God to be eternal ("which was, and is, and is to come"). God has always been, and always will be. His holiness and power will never diminish, because He would cease to exist if they did. God will always rule, as He always has. He will never be defeated, never be beaten. He is the one and only Lord God Almighty.

The twenty-four elders remind us that God created everything. They also reveal to us the fact that everything was created for His pleasure. So, if something is not pleasing God, or even hurting Him, would He not have the right to destroy it? This earth which has been overrun by sin is not pleasing to God. It is not the earth He created and intended it to be. Should He not then just destroy it? And what about mankind? We sin against God, and shake our puny fists at Him in hatred and defiance, and turn our backs in disbelief. Should He not have the right to destroy us? Of course the Creator has the right to destroy what He has created. Everything we see, and don't see, is God's. It was created by Him, and is owned by Him, and he can do whatever He wants with His own possessions.

Chapter five of Revelation brings in another Character, and reveals another aspect of God. We see a Lamb who has been slain. It is kind of a grotesque mutation with seven horns and seven eyes, but as we read further, we realize that this is Jesus. Why did Jesus die? Verse nine gives the story in a nutshell. Jesus died so that people could have a relationship with God. It is the blood of Jesus that brings us into relationship with God.

But, why was the death of Jesus necessary? When we sin, we do things that God would not do. We do not listen to, or follow, God's definition of what is right and wrong. Instead, we come up with our own definitions, or allow someone else to set the standard.

Whenever we listen to someone else instead of God, and act accordingly, justice must step in and pronounce a death sentence. That sounds harsh, but let me explain. Death is simply a matter of separation. Our soul/spirit separates from our physical body and it is called physical death. When our soul/spirit separates from God, it is called spiritual death.

As we refuse to listen to God and choose our own standards of right and wrong, it creates a barrier between us and God. Remember how we like to hide our dark side? But, it also puts us in a position where we are not willing to be around God because we want to do our own thing. We would rather be separated from God than have a relationship with Him.

Justice actually demands that we continue to be separated from God for eternity. Even with our first venture into trying to decide things for ourselves, we pull away from God. This is a tendency that will never change because we are human. The ultimate end is an eternity spent away from God. So, justice demands that even the smallest sin be dealt the death penalty of eternal separation from God.

But, God created us to have a relationship with Him. Separation from God was the penalty for sin. So, what was God going to do? Only one thing could allow people to come into a relationship with God. One person would have to live a sinless life, and then willingly die to pay the price for everyone else. You see, if a person never sinned, then they would not deserve to die, even physically, so they would have to give up their life.

No one, no person, could ever live up to that requirement of perfection. The human race was doomed to spend an eternity in the lake of fire. But God knew what people would do even before He created them. He had a plan long before the earth was ever formed and He created man. God Himself, as Jesus, would come to earth as a man and live a perfect life. He would give up His life, be slain, in order to bring us back into a relationship with Himself. The holiness and justice of God would be satisfied. One, Who did not deserve it, died in place of those who did deserve death. And all God asks is that we accept this.

> As we go through this book we will talk about accepters and refusers. An accepter is a person who has accepted the fact that Jesus had to die to pay the price for sin. This person has entered into a relationship with Jesus. A refuser on the other hand, is a person who refuses to accept the fact that Jesus died for him. This person refuses to allow Jesus into his life. (See Appendix A, An Accepter's Story.)

We saw God's holiness displayed in chapter four, but here in chapter five we see His grace. Grace is receiving what we do not deserve. We do not deserve an eternal relationship with God, and yet He made the way for it to be given to us. God revealing His holiness and then His grace is not unusual. We have already mentioned the experiences of Isaiah and Moses when they met God. God showed His grace to Isaiah by placing a coal on his lips and forgiving him of his sin. God displayed his grace to Moses by revealing the way He was going to free the people of Israel from Egyptian slavery.

I think it is unfortunate that too many authors and speakers on future events skip over this section of scripture in Revelation. They may talk about all the symbolism, but they fail to see the revealing of the holiness and grace of God.

These two concepts give us a greater understanding of the events we will study.

It is God's holiness that boils over into the tribulation period in a conflict with evil and a final attempt to get man to turn to good. Plague after plague is placed on the earth and its inhabitants in a relentless barrage. It is God's holiness which rules the great white throne judgment, and which creates the lake of fire in which refusers spend eternity. We study about events like these and they run counter to what most of us think about God. We ask the simple question, how could a God of love do something like this? But, the real question is, how can a God of holiness not do something like this? It is actually loving of God to give people a final chance to accept what He has done for them instead of just wiping them out without warning.

While God's holiness is on the rampage during the final events of this universe, His grace is also at full throttle. God still gives people chances to enter into a relationship with Him. He provides two witnesses who will speak the truth about Jesus during the first part of the tribulation. There will be 144,000 Jewish believers who accept Jesus during the tribulation period and spread the gospel to the whole world. A great multitude of people will become accepters during this period in history. And, just when we think it is over, God gives people one final chance to truly decide whether to accept or refuse Him at the end of the millennial kingdom. The God of grace gives people many chances to come to Him.

Looking at future events forces us to look at a part of God we do not like to think about. Yet, we cannot truly appreciate the grace God has given us if we do not understand His holiness. God's holiness would be fully justified in taking all of the accepters out of this world, leaving only the refusers, and then unloading His wrath and fury with no more chances for people to turn to Him. But His grace gives more chances.

> We cannot fully understand the grace of people entering into a relationship with God during the tribulation period without understanding the holiness behind the wrath and fury.

We could spend volumes discussing the importance and relevance of holiness and grace to future, as well as present, events. So, let us move on. We have seen Jesus as the Lamb Who was slain, but it is not just the sacrificial death of Jesus, but His resurrection that is important. Jesus was in the grave for three days. I am sure that during that time Satan was trying to find something against Jesus that would force God to leave Him dead in the tomb. Nothing could be found. Jesus had lived a perfect life in relation to God. Satan lost, and Jesus was restored back to life.

The resurrection of Jesus is very important to future events. As we will see, there are some prophecies concerning Jesus that have not been fulfilled. The resurrection of Jesus is the hinge of all prophecy. Old Testament prophets saw a Messiah, a Savior, Who would come and die for the sin of the world. At the same time, they saw this same person ruling from the land of Israel as a King over all the earth. These two visions of the Messiah would be impossible if it were not for the resurrection. Jesus came the first time to fulfill the prophecies of being the sacrifice for the world. He will come again to complete the prophecies by being King.

We have looked into the throne room of God and have seen the prelude to the future events. We have seen this awesome, powerful God who is holy, and the slain Lamb Who died to display the grace of this same God. Jesus bore the full wrath of God's justice through death so that we would not have to, and so that we could have a relationship with God. But, those who refuse God will have to bear the consequences during the events yet to come.

READ: DEUTERONOMY 18:20–22

There is something very important we must learn from the above scripture. Within this passage God is giving the nation of Israel directions for how to spot a true prophet. He is telling them the qualifications for a person who says they know the future. If the qualifications are met, then the people are to listen to this person. But, if they are not met, then that person is to die.

There are really two standards that God sets in this matter. First, the person must speak in the name of the true God. In other words, if someone says they know the future, they must at least claim to be receiving their information from God. Second, all of their predictions must be 100% accurate. If they claim to be speaking for God, then they have to be 100% accurate because God does not make mistakes.

Why are these two rules important? First, only God accurately knows the future. To rely on any other source could cause us to have misinformation. Second, if the person foretelling the future is not accurate, how does he hold any credibility?

Think of it this way. United States currency is good because it is backed by the government of the United States. I can go anywhere in the U.S. and pay my bills with U.S. currency. However, foreign money, while backed by a government, is not readily accepted. The stability of the source is not as well known in the United States. A counterfeit bill has no value at all, because there is no government backing it.

When dealing with people who tell the future, we must know who is backing them. What is their source of information? God says that anything not backed by Him is unreliable at best and a forgery at worst. Just like we have a hard time taking foreign currency or a counterfeit bill, we must be wary of people who profess to know the future, but do not cite God as their source for information.

In order to have credibility the government always has to honor its debt in backing currency. Otherwise, we would never know if the dollar bill we had was worth anything or not. In the same way, the predictions about the future that are said to come from God must be 100% accurate. Anything less would always have us wondering if it was truth or not.

As we study future events in this book, we will be looking at authors who meet these criteria. They speak because God told them to speak, and they have shown a pattern of accuracy so far. The Old Testament prophets made predictions about Israel going into captivity, and returning from it. They predicted the coming of Jesus to die for the sin of the world. All of those predictions have come true with 100% accuracy. This gives us confidence in what they have predicted about our future.

The Apostle John, who wrote the book of Revelation, does not have the track record of the Old Testament prophets. However, most of his prophecies are bolstered by the prophecies of the Old Testament. He simply fills in some details. Up to this point, there is no reason to believe that John has been wrong, or will be wrong, about anything he predicted. He does say that this revelation of future events was given to him directly by God.

READ: 1 THESSALONIANS 5:5–11

Why should we study future events? One of the things I have realized in studying the passages of scripture about the end times is that, God would not have given us this look into the future unless it would affect the way we live in the here and now. In other words, God did not show us the future just to satisfy our curiosity. He had a life changing reason that was to be applied to the present.

It is this life changing element that makes Bible prophecy different from others who predict the future. In the Old Testament God told the people of Israel and Judah that they were going to be taken into captivity. He did this as a warning. This future forecast was given to them to encourage them to change the way they were living. They were worshipping gods other than the true God. They were becoming depraved in their morality. God warned them to change their ways, or they would suffer the consequences. He wanted them to change their lifestyle at that moment, not after the captivity started. God gives us a glimpse into our future so that it will change the way we live today.

In the passage you just read the Apostle Paul is writing to the church in Thessalonica, a city in Asia-minor. This church had been suffering from the false teaching that Jesus had already come again to collect the accepters, and they missed it. They thought they had been left behind. This caused some to doubt their faith. Paul gives them a brief teaching about the coming of Jesus, future events, and then concludes with the passage you read. He gives them practical, everyday reasons why it is important to know the truth about the return of Jesus.

First, he tells them in verse six to not be lax morally, but to be aware of their present surroundings and not let sin sneak up on them. They were to be sober, self-controlled, in a morally lax society so that they could resist temptation. If Jesus is coming, and He is, then we do not want Him to find us in a lax moral state. We want to be found representing Him well in this world and living a life that is drawing us closer to God instead of pushing us away from God.

Imagine yourself as a child at home when your parents are out for the evening. You do not know when they will be home. They have left specific instructions that you are not to watch a certain movie that is coming on television that night. You are torn. You want to watch the movie, but you are not sure when your parents will be home. They might catch you watching the movie. The fact that you do not want to be caught is motivation to not watch the movie. In the same way, we should expect Jesus to come at any time. We would not want to be caught doing something He would disapprove of when He arrives.

Next, in verse eight, Paul tells the church that looking forward to the future events should help us live with faith and love, and bolster the hope of our salvation. We know what Jesus has done for us through His death on the cross, and now we can see what the future holds for us. If God was faithful in fulfilling His promise to pay the price so we can have an eternal relationship with Him, then He will also be faithful in fulfilling Jesus' promise to return for us. Our past experience should support our faith of the future. If we are trusting God for the big thing, our future, then we should be able to live our lives by trusting God for the small, every-day things.

To the accepter, the revealing of future events is really a revelation of God's love and grace to him. We can easily see how much God loves us because of the place He has created for us to spend an eternity. We know of His love because He is going to spend eternity with us. We know Jesus loves us because He is returning to get us so we can be with Him. The love we know to be true in God is poured out into our life, even today. We should therefore spread that love to others around us.

Part of the future events we will study will be what happens to refusers. There is a place called the lake of fire where refusers will spend eternity. God has made it clear by showing us the future that accepters will not be subjected to such torment. Our hope is God and an eternity with Him in love. That hope should bring a smile to our face, and a peace to our heart, whenever we remember it. It should also make us determined to share the truth about Jesus with others, so they will have the same hope in their life.

Finally, Paul tells the Thessalonians to comfort each other, and build each other up, by thinking about the promised future. When times are hard we can look to the promises God has given us by showing us the future and find comfort and strength. We have something to look forward to that is better than what we are presently experiencing. The churches Paul dealt with were suffering from persecution by the Roman government. They were afraid of torture and death. But, the thought of heaven, and even of God getting revenge on their enemies, was a comfort, and would give them strength to endure the suffering. Paul considered this such an important point that he emphasized it again in his second letter to this church (2 Thessalonians 2:1–2).

The Apostle Peter, in his second letter, gives us a final reason to study and learn about the coming events (2 Peter 3:10–18). Peter describes the destruction of the physical universe by fire. Then he asks the question, "If all these things are going to be burned up, how should you be living your life?" Obviously everything that we work for, like money and property, is going to be burned up. What does that leave you? Peter is basically saying that how we live is very important. Our view of the future should make us want to live holy lives; lives full of goodness. It should make us want to be more like God in doing what is right. It should make us want to grow in our knowledge of the grace of God, and in the sacrifice Jesus made for us.

Simply put, we should know about future events so we will be better people. This study should make us want to draw closer to God, praise Him for our salvation, and become more like Him. It should help deepen our faith and trust in God. Thinking about the future should lift us up when we are down. Knowing about what is yet to take place should keep our priorities in this life on the right track. Knowing the fate of accepters and refusers should drive us to share the love and salvation of Jesus with others. I believe God had good reasons for sharing the future with us.

***** PROCEED WITH CAUTION *****

As we enter into our study of future events we must be cautious. The study of Bible prophecy has some traps into which some people fall. Hopefully by discussing some of these pit-falls up front, we will not be as likely to step into them and get hurt.

Prophecies about future events are subject to interpretation.

Interpretation is simply coming up with what you think something means. It is usually based on a lot of factors, including what preconceived ideas you bring to the subject matter, and experience with the subject matter. As we look at a passage you may see something totally different than I see. This could be because I have done more study and am relating something else I know to the passage, whereas this is the first time you have ever seen the passage. I know my interpretations of some passages have changed over time as I have grown in my knowledge and experience, and have been able to relate a passage more to the whole subject instead of just a part.

People come with preconceived ideas as well. If you have ever studied this topic before, then you already have a preconceived idea. There is a wide variety of opinions out there in regards to interpretation. It is usually easy to spot the wild ideas, most are laughable, but it is not so easy to spot some of the more subtle errors in interpretation. Some of our preconceived ideas are derived from error, either on our part or the part of others who have taught us. As they say, been there, done that. I have had to change some of my preconceived notions about certain portions of prophetic events as I have studied.

The best way to keep away from the pit-fall of preconceived ideas and wrong interpretation is to remember a couple of rules. First, the best interpreter of scripture is scripture. If the Bible gives an explanation about what something means, then that is what it means. For instance, in Daniel chapters seven and eight, Daniel relates visions he had of the future. The interpretation of these visions is then spelled out for us in those chapters. Jesus would sometimes give the interpretation of His parables to the disciples. When the Bible gives an interpretation, then we do not need to look any further. No one else is going to be able to come up with a better interpretation than the Bible can for itself.

Of course, there are times when the Bible does not give us an interpretation. When this is true, and the passage is not easily understood, then we must refrain from being dogmatic in our interpretation. We must allow grace toward other interpretations, as long as they do not do damage to other scriptures. If an interpretation is counter to the teaching of any other scripture, then that interpretation is wrong. Scripture will never contradict itself! But, if there is no damage done to other scriptures, and the Bible does not give a clear interpretation, then we must not hold our interpretation as the only answer. We must be cautious because our interpretation may change over time as we learn more facts. What this boils down to is, when the Bible is silent, one person's interpretation may be as good as another. If the opinions oppose each other they cannot both be right, but they could both be wrong. We need to show grace toward those who have a different opinion.

Most future events are spiritual in nature.

Some people give man too much credit for instigating future events. They read through the books of Daniel and Revelation, and see man destroying himself. We need to remember that the future events we are about to study are orchestrated by God for a specific purpose. It is God exerting His holiness and trying to convince men to turn away from the destructive evil they have been embracing.

Man does not bring the plagues of the tribulation period on himself. God sends them. Man does not destroy the earth with nuclear bombs. God destroys the earth, and the heavens with His own power. While man may be used in some instances, the battle is the Lord's. It is God versus Satan and man, not man versus man. Some interpretations of Revelation have sought to put airplanes and tanks and modern weapons of warfare in place of supernatural beings directed by God. Yet, the Bible gives every indication that what is being described is a supernatural warfare waged by God. To some extent it is like saying the plagues of Egypt during the time of Moses were brought on by chemical warfare and radiation mutations.

As we study it is important for us to remember that it is God who is instigating all of these things. Satan is doing his thing in trying to defeat God's plan, but God is using him to fulfill it. You have two spiritual heavy weights fighting it out, with physical man in the middle trying to decide which side to join. The weapons of mass destruction in our modern arsenals are nothing compared to what God has in His arsenal. So, we are going to give the benefit of the doubt to God when it comes to the weapons, and even warriors, we see as we study. Of course though, this is one of those areas where we must allow for grace in interpretation by others.

Many prophecies of future events are eyewitness accounts, which are not chronological, but accurate.

The best example of this statement is the book of Revelation. The Apostle John is trying to relate everything he is seeing. He is in the position of a news commentator. Today, if a major event happens in the world, the news agencies will have a team of reporters covering different angles of the same story. This is basically John's position as he is writing. When we read Revelation we think John is skipping around a lot and getting sidetracked. Actually, he is just trying to convey the events of a seven-year period by giving different perspectives. He focuses on different people and events, and sometimes has to start over from the beginning to allow us to see what this person does, or how this event took shape.

It is also a part of the Mid-East mindset to group things together. In the western culture we think of things as being one after another, or linear. But, the oriental, Mid-East, mindset tends to group like things together. That is why the books of the Bible are arranged the way they are. Books are grouped together by the books Moses authored, history, poetry and wisdom, and prophecy. They are not in chronological order. Neither is the book of Revelation.

While John may not have been able to relate the events in pure chronological order, all that he relates is accurate in description. We cannot discount anything John says simply because it does not follow a logical order like we would want it. Nor, should we give up studying it because we have trouble following the plot. John wasn't writing a novel, he was writing a news story. God was the one giving John the information, and God decided the order it would be given and written. So, do not get discouraged if you find some prophecy hard to follow, everyone has that problem.

The prophecies of future events do not tell us everything.

In Revelation 10:3–4, John is forbidden to write what the seven thunders said. We are left to speculate. These may be another series of plagues on the earth, or just statements about something going on in heaven. We do not know, and God did not want us to know. Apparently God wants to be able to hold a few tricks up His sleeve that people are not expecting.

This should humble us. Only God knows exactly what is going to happen in the future. We know enough to want to avoid it, but we do not know everything.

If someone declares that they know everything that is going to happen during the seven year tribulation period, they are lying and have no credibility.

It is interesting that God even allowed us to know that there were seven thunders who spoke, and that John was not allowed to write down what was said. Quite possibly God did want to make the very important point that we have not been told everything. Who knows what God did not reveal to John? As we study future events, we must always remember that there are gaps in our knowledge, either because of our lack of knowledge, or because God simply has not revealed it to us.

Well, we have placed the first things first. We looked at the importance of understanding the holiness and grace of God as it relates to future events. It is the holiness of God, His repulsion to sin because of the consequences to us, that boils over into the plagues of the last days and the destruction of the universe. But, it is the grace of God, through Jesus, that gives people another chance at entering into an eternal relationship with God, even in the middle of His anger against sin. We also saw several, practical reasons for studying future events. Our knowledge and attitude toward future events has a profound influence on our every day life, especially spiritually. And, finally, we looked at some things to be cautious of when studying Bible prophecy concerning future events.

MIND THE GAP

There are only two groups of people in the world, accepters and refusers. When we study future events we see the ultimate consequences to our choice.

I was privileged to be a part of a group from my church that went to England to help facilitate a leadership conference for church leaders. If you go to England, you must ride their Underground, which is what we would call a subway. It is a very convenient and economical form of transportation. It was a challenge getting all ten of us on and off the trains at the same time while toting more luggage than we would have liked. Sometimes it was amusing, usually it was not.

There was something that did amuse us whenever we heard it. A voice over the station's loudspeaker would say "Mind the gap. Mind the gap." This was repeated whenever a train was to arrive or depart in order to remind the people of the danger of the gap between the train and the platform. Apparently we are not the first tourists to find this announcement somewhat amusing. Some of the shops sell signs and t-shirts with "MIND THE GAP" on them.

We were in England for several days. The more we heard "Mind the gap," the more the significance of the phrase began to sink in. The reason we were there was to train church leaders, and help them grow in their leadership skills. Why? Because, we know the importance of a strong and healthy church in connecting people to God.

There is a gap between God and humans that must be minded. The church is to point people to the truth of how to mind that gap. If you fail to mind the gap between the platform and the train, you may fall and break your leg. But, if you fail to mind the gap between you and God, you will spend an eternity in worse suffering than you can imagine.

Toward the end of the trip it was hard not to look at the people boarding the train and wonder. They are so mindful of that gap so they do not fall; how mindful are they of the gap between them and God?

All ten of us crammed into a vendor's little shop that really should have only held about two people, and bought "MIND THE GAP" t-shirts. We wear them and remember. "Mind the gap" is not as amusing as it once was. In fact, it is serious business.

Looks
Like
This
Is
The
End

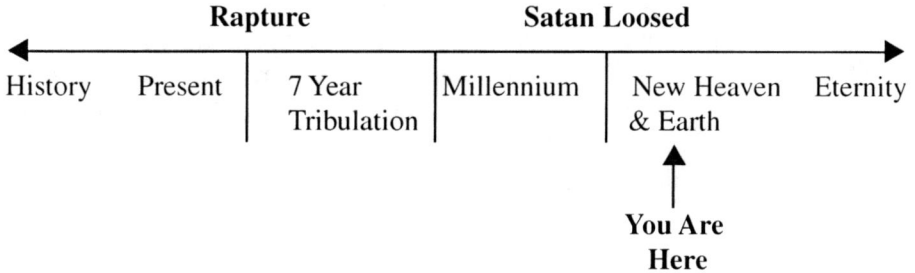

> **READ:** REVELATION 21:1–22:5

Even if they do not believe in it, most people at least hope there is a heaven, a place that is far better than life on this earth, where they can go when they die. The Bible describes such a place. Jesus talked about it in His final words to His disciples on the night He was betrayed (John 14:1–3). The Apostle John was given a glimpse of it when He was shown what the end times are to be like (Revelation 21, 22). John saw the final dwelling place for those who have accepted God's payment for their sin. It is called the new heaven and new earth (Revelation 21:1).

"New" is the key word in Revelation 21:1. The verse goes on to say that the old earth and heaven have gone away. What happened to them that new ones had to be created? Peter gives the description of what happens in 2 Peter 3:10–13. He says that the earth we know now, and the heavens (sky, space) will be burned up, will melt with extreme heat. Then God will create new ones. Why would God do this? Because the earth and all of creation has been tainted by sin. God wants a place for us that is perfect, just like He created at first with Adam and Eve in the Garden of Eden (Genesis 1–3).

John implies in Revelation that heaven itself, the place where we believe God now dwells, will also be destroyed and a new heaven formed. So, why would God destroy everything, including heaven, which is perfect? The answer, I think, is found in Revelation 21:3, 22. In these verses it is clear that God is going to physically live with those who have accepted Him. This means there are going to have to be some real changes in the way the universe works.

As it stands now there are two worlds, the physical and the spiritual. In the very beginning there was only God, a spirit being. God then created other spirit beings we call angels, and heaven, a spiritual realm where they could live. Then He created something totally new, a physical place with physical beings called humans. These two realms do not mix. The physical cannot live in the spiritual, and the spiritual cannot live in the physical, without something changing.

God's ultimate plan is to physically live with those He loves. So, He destroys the current physical and spiritual realms and creates a brand new realm that combines both in a perfect way. The resurrection body of Jesus is a glimpse of what people will be like in this new heaven and earth combined. After His resurrection Jesus could enter closed rooms (John 20:19), yet He could be touched by others and eat food (Luke 24:36–43). Jesus was now a combination of both the spiritual and physical world. Paul describes this new body that will live in the new heaven and earth, and how the body we now have must be changed in order to live there with God as physical/spiritual beings (1 Corinthians 15:35–58).

At this time heaven is a place where the soul/spirit of those who have accepted God's payment for their sin live. Paul says in 2 Corinthians 5:8 that he wants to be absent from this body and present with the Lord. That means that when a person dies, their soul/spirit separates itself from this body, which is left behind on earth. The soul/spirit of accepters of Jesus go to be with Him, in the place we call heaven. According to Paul, these soul/spirits will one day be reunited with their bodies, but the bodies will be changed to live in the new heaven and earth. Heaven and earth will become one as God creates His new place for everyone to live with Him forever.

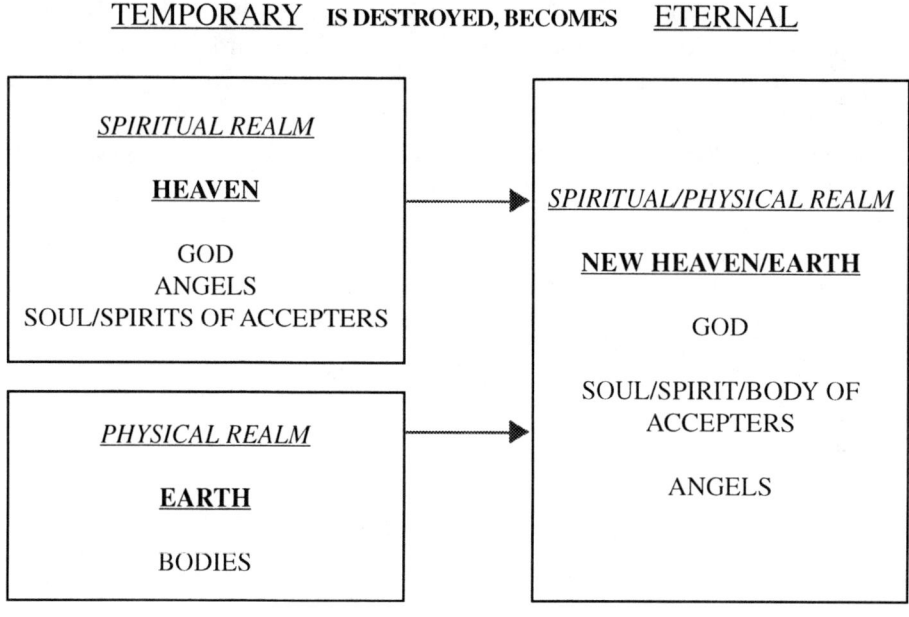

Eternity is a long time, and that is how long this new heaven and earth will last. We will be living with God forever (Revelation 22:5, 1 Thessalonians 4:17). When most people think about an eternity in heaven, they see themselves dressed in white, sitting on a cloud, playing a harp forever. I'm sorry, but I believe that would be boring, and God does not do boring.

When God created man the first time, He gave man a job, a purpose for living. Man was to tend to the garden (Genesis 1:28; 2:15). In Revelation we see that man is to serve God and reign on the earth. And, we see that people will live outside of the actual city of New Jerusalem (21:24). These people will bring the glory and honor of the nations into the city. In other words, work will be done which will bring glory to God.

In 1 Corinthians 12:4–11, Paul says that gifts, abilities, are given to those who accept God by the Spirit of God. These gifts and abilities are to be used to promote God, and to help the church as a whole grow in its knowledge of God and bring others to a knowledge of God. Some of the gifts God gives through His Spirit are administration, knowledge, discernment of truth, the ability to be a help and a comfort to others, and the ability to be hospitable. God gives gifts, and He also provides people with talents. Accepters of God are not the only ones with talents. Many people can sing, some write books, others are great artists or poets, and some are good with math, or gardening, or science. God gives us gifts and talents to be used here on earth, why would He take all that away and relegate us all to just playing the harp when we get to heaven?

Allow me to propose a hypothesis. The gifts and talents we have been given here will be far more advanced when we get to heaven. There are good reasons to believe this.

- God is not a God of boredom. He created this world with variety, and gives us interesting things to experience, how much more would He do that with a perfect world.
- Gifts have been given by the Holy Spirit, Whose influence will be even stronger in the new heaven and earth than it is now. Therefore the gifts will be much more perfected.
- We will be serving God, therefore we will need to use the gifts and talents He has provided.
- The best way to learn about God is to have experiences. If all we do all day is sit around strumming a harp, we will not experience much of God.
- One of the greatest pleasures in life is a job well done. God would not deprive us of that for eternity, especially when the jobs will be for Him.
- As we look at the descriptions of this new heaven and earth, there are places to live, a street to walk on, a river to cross or swim in, and fruit to eat. There is work to be done. Even the angels now are at work. The new heaven and earth is going to be alive with activity.

We will not be bored and inactive for eternity. I believe that there will be those who study the new creation just as scientists today study this one. But, they will have a true grasp of truth. Explorers will explore an infinite new creation. Musicians will write new, awesome tunes to praise God. Artists will have new, more perfect forms of art to express their love for the Creator. Books will be written and read, gardens grown, and buildings constructed. There will even be animals there. (The armies of heaven have horses Revelation 19:14.) How awesome will eternity be with God as the center of all these activities?

The New Jerusalem is the centerpiece of the new heaven and new earth. It is where God will physically dwell. God's greatest desire is fulfilled as he creates a place to live with those He loves (Revelation 21:3).

John gives us as good a description as possible of the New Jerusalem. He sees it coming out of heaven from God. It is basically clear as the walls of the city are made of a crystal like mineral, which allows the light coming from within to pass through it. It has twelve gates guarded by twelve angels, and twelve foundations of various stones. The city is 1500 miles wide, long and high. To put that in a little perspective, that is like drawing a line through Kansas City, Missouri from the Canadian border to about the middle of Texas, then going all the way to the California coast to complete the square. That's the length and width. Tip that square on its end and you would have the height. Talk about big! The throne of God is found in this city, and a river runs from it. There is a street of gold, and the tree of life (which was removed from earth after Adam and Eve sinned) is found there. God's presence lights everything, so there will never be night again.

The new heaven and earth is the ultimate of God's expression of grace. None of us deserves to be in such a beautiful place. None of us deserves to live with God. Without God's intervention in our lives through Jesus, God's justice would have barred us from being with Him. But God loves us so much that He made a place where we can live with Him, not for just a few short years, but for eternity. And, He did not skimp on the building materials. The new heaven and earth is perfect in beauty, far more than we deserve.

Revelation 21:7, 8 tells us that this city, this new Jerusalem, is only for those who have accepted God's work for them, through Jesus. Everyone else, those who have refused God's payment for their sin, are to be put into a lake of fire. This brings us to the subject of hell. There will be a new heaven and a new earth, there will also be a new hell, called the lake of fire.

What is hell today? Well, just like heaven is a temporary holding place of the soul/spirit for those who have accepted Jesus, until they are reunited with their bodies and the new heaven and earth are created, hell is the temporary holding place for the soul/spirit of those who have refused Jesus.

The Bible does talk a lot about hell, and it is always described as a place that is burning and dark and causes torment. Jesus told a story in Luke 16 about a rich man who went to hell and suffered torment. He begged for a drop of water to touch his tongue, but it was not given. He also begged to be able to go tell his family about where they were headed so they would change their ways and avoid hell, but that was not granted either.

No one can say for certain where hell is now. Some people think that hell is at the center of the earth; others think it is just a different dimension. What we do know is that it is a temporary holding place for soul/spirits who have refused God, and that it is a place of torment.

But, why would God create such a place, and then create a permanent place such as the lake of fire? Jesus gives us the answer in Matthew 25:41. Hell was created for the devil and his angels. Satan rebelled against God. He thought he should be in power instead of God. Satan did not want God to rule over him, or be a part of his life, and he convinced other angels to think the same way. It would have been cruel for God to force Satan and his angels to live where they did not want to be, so, God created a place where Satan and his followers could live without His presence in their lives. The problem is, as James 1:17 tells us, that everything good comes from God. So, if you remove God, you remove everything that is good. All you have left is evil and torment, which is what hell is.

That is why today we have a pocket somewhere in the physical or spiritual universe where God does not make His presence known. It is evil, dark, and tormenting with heat. The soul/spirit of every person who refuses to accept God into their life is placed in this pocket and kept there until they will be reunited with their body to be cast into the lake of fire for eternity. Not really something to look forward to, is it?

The lake of fire is the ultimate expression of God's holiness. Only the holiness of God could create a place where a person would never have to experience the presence of God. Remember, holiness has no place for evil, and it seeks to keep us from experiencing the negative consequences evil produces. In His holiness God has confined all the evil to one place in the universe, forever separating those who follow God from the negative consequences it produces. As close as accepters are to God in the new heaven and earth through grace, refusers will be separated from God through holiness.

MIND THE GAP

I mentioned the story Jesus told in Luke 16 about the rich man and Lazarus. This story actually went against the predominant belief of Jesus' time. Most people believed that the rich were blessed by God and the poor were cursed by God. Therefore, a rich person had to be a lock for an eternity in heaven, while a poor person was destined for hell. But, in His story, Jesus said that the rich man went to hell and the poor man went to heaven.

There is a truth here that we must not miss. It is not our social status that decides where we will spend eternity; it is our relationship with God. We choose what path we wish to follow. Ultimately, each individual decides where he or she will spend eternity. Being born into a wealthy family, or in a prosperous country, does not mean you are blessed by God and are going to heaven. At the same time, being born into poverty, or a third world country, does not mean that God is cursing you and you are doomed to an eternity in hell. It is our choice to love God and accept Him in our life that is the determining factor.

Another point we must not miss is found when the rich man realizes the truth mentioned above. He desperately wants to share this information with his family. He wants to be able to go to them and tell them that they are not getting into heaven just because they are rich. Unfortunately, he found out the truth too late. There was nothing he could do to tell his family.

However, accepters know the same truth as the rich man. We must have the same reaction. We must want to share it with others so they will not have to suffer. Fortunately, accepters have learned this truth while there is still something that can be done about it.

Because the church knows the final destination of both accepters and refusers, we are motivated to reach out to the refusers. The church must declare the truth to show refusers the importance of each person minding the gap between them and God.

READ: REVELATION 20:11–15

According to what we just read there is coming a day of judgment. There will be a great white throne where God sits to judge people. Actually, John 5:22 tells us that all judgment is given over to the Son, Jesus. So, it is probably Jesus, Who is God, Who is on the throne. Apparently, at this time, heaven and earth are destroyed. John describes it as the heaven and earth fleeing from the face of Jesus on the throne.

John sees the dead standing before God. Social status does not matter, the rich are not going to be excused because they are powerful, and the poor will not be excused out of sympathy. All the dead at this time will stand before God to be judged.

It is important here to define who is considered "dead". Physical death can be defined as the separation of the soul/spirit from the body. When a person dies on earth, their soul/spirit separates from their body and either goes to heaven or hell, while their body remains here to be cremated or buried. So, all who appear at this judgment will be people whose body and soul/spirit have not yet been reunited. They are still physically dead.

We know that the soul/spirit and the body are still separated at this time because John describes their coming together in verse 13. The sea gave up its dead, meaning all the bodies from the ocean, and death gave up its dead. We can say that death is another term for the state of those bodies in the grave on land, which are separated from their soul/spirit. Hell gives up its dead, which are the soul/spirits of those who have refused to allow God into their life. The bodies from the land and sea meet up with the soul/spirits from hell, are joined together, and stand before God to be judged.

As these people stand there, once again a complete person with soul/spirit joined with body, there are some books opened. According to verse 12, these people are judged by what is written in the books, and what is written is the works they have done while alive on earth. These people are being judged by their own works to see how they measure up to the perfection of God. Of course, no one is going to pass this judgment because no one can measure up to perfection. It is the justice of God that rules this trial, not grace, or even mercy. The final book is the Book of Life. When their name is not found there, then they are condemned to an eternity in the lake of fire.

THE BOOK OF LIFE

READ THESE SCRIPTURES

Psalm 69:28 Book of Life with names of the righteous
Revelation 13:8 Book of Life of the Lamb—Being of the Lamb (in Christ) is being righteous
Exodus 32:33 God's Book—blots out those who have sinned
Revelation 3:5 Book of Life—Righteous will not be blotted out
Revelation 21:27 Lamb's Book of Life Sinner's not in, Righteous are

There has been some confusion over the Book of Life mentioned in Revelation 20:15, as it relates to other mentions of a book in other passages of scripture. We have just looked at the other passages where a book of life is mentioned by another name. Some people hold that these are different books, but I believe that the evidence is clear that they are the same book.

All of the books mentioned contain the names of the righteous, who will spend eternity with God. Sometimes the scripture mentions the unrighteous being blotted out, sometimes it talks about the righteous being left in. Either way, the righteous have their names in the book, and those who are not in the book will have to spend eternity away from God. To put it into the terms we have been using, those who accept God into their life have their names in the book, those who refuse God are blotted out of the book.

The change from the book being God's Book, where God the Father has the right to blot people out in Exodus, to the Lamb's Book of Life, where Jesus has the authority to place people in or take them out in Revelation, is easily explained. We have already looked at James 5:22, which says that all judgment has been given to the Son. Because of His sacrifice for us, God has given Jesus the authority over the Book, hence, the name change.

Who are these people who are standing before God at this judgment? We have several clues from the passage (Revelation 20:15). First, they are people who have not yet had their soul/spirit reunited with their body. This does not tell us much at this stage of our study, but will become very important later.

Second, they are people whose soul/spirit is in hell, the temporary holding place for those who have refused God in their life. Notice that only hell has given up its dead, not heaven (13). This means that only refusers are standing in this judgment before Jesus, the very person they refused to allow into their life.

Third, these people are judged by their works to determine their eternal destiny. Those who accept Jesus are judged by the works of Jesus for their eternal destiny, not their own works. Look at Ephesians 2:4–9. God looks at accepters through Jesus, and His work on the cross to pay for our sin. They are not saved by works, and are not judged by their works, but are saved and judged by the works of Jesus. Therefore, no accepters are in this judgment.

Finally, Revelation 20:15, somewhat implies that no one who was a part of this judgment was found to have their name written in the Book of Life. All were cast into the lake of fire for eternity. This is not a very strong argument by itself, but placed with the other arguments it lends strength to the conclusion. The only people who are judged at the great white throne judgment are refusers.

We also note that death and hell are cast into the lake of fire. Both of these are temporary. Hell is the temporary holding place of the soul/spirit, and death is the temporary state of the body separated from the soul/spirit. Both of these will cease to exist as the lake of fire now becomes the permanent residence of the reunited soul/spirit/body. We also mentioned that hell had been created for the Devil and his angels. They will also be placed into the lake of fire so they can spend eternity without God.

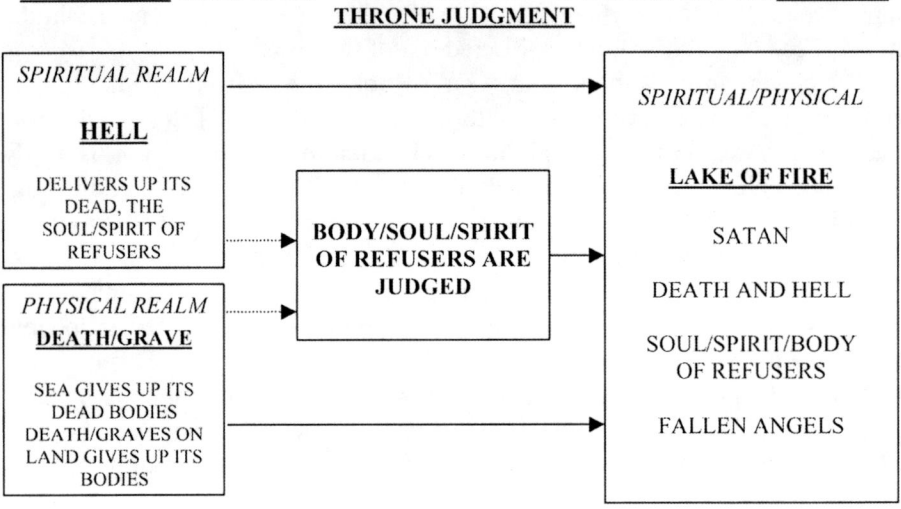

Verse 14 mentions the second death. The first death is the separation of the soul/spirit from the body, and that is temporary. The second death is total separation from God, and that is eternal.

MIND THE GAP

The passage we read in Revelation 20:11–15 is sobering. It shows us three things very clearly. First, it shows us that there will be a judgment before God. The author of the book of Hebrews in the New Testament said that man will die once, and then receive judgment (Hebrews 9:27). No one escapes judgment. As we continue on with our study, we will see a judgment of accepters.

Second, these people were judged by their works (Revelation 20:12). The books contained a record of each and every action made by the person being judged. The standard to meet is perfection. In order to be condemned at this trial a person only had to do one action that would cause a negative consequence either to him or to someone else. No one could stand up to that. Also, the biggest action that causes a negative consequence is refusing a relationship with God. On that act alone they can be, and will be, condemned. To refuse God is to choose an eternal life without Him. It is to choose eternal torment.

Third, we see that there are no final chances to choose God after death. The soul/spirit of these people went straight from hell to be rejoined with their body for this judgment. There was no asking if these people had changed their minds and wanted a relationship with God. They were judged by their works alone. The final cut off for deciding to have a relationship with God is before you die. After that, you will either stand in the judgment with refusers, or with accepters.

Our works are not enough to obtain an eternal relationship with God. The saying that "nobody is perfect" is true. That is what the people of the Great White Throne Judgment find out. There is death and then there is judgment. There is no making amends in hell. This is why accepters struggle so much to find ways to relate the truth to those who are currently refusing God. We never know when death will end a person's chances to enter into a relationship with God.

SUMMARY

In this chapter we have looked at what the final end is going to be for the people of this earth. We learned that there are two temporary holding places for the soul/spirit of people. Which holding place the soul/spirit goes depends on accepting or refusing God. Those who accept God into their life go to heaven, those who refuse God go to hell. The temporary holding place for the bodies is on earth, either land or sea.

These temporary holding places will be destroyed and replaced with new, eternal places. There will be a new heaven and earth for the accepters, and a lake of fire for the refusers. These new places will be populated with the reunited soul/spirit/body.

Finally, we learned that there will be a judgment of the refusers at the great white throne of God. Jesus, the one they refused, will be the judge. They will be judged by their works, which will fail to get them into heaven when compared to the perfect holiness of God. Their names will have been taken out of the Book of Life, and they are then condemned to spend eternity in the lake of fire.

If we know what the end is for people, should we not be doing something to make sure that we are going to heaven? And, once we are certain about our destination, should we not be concerned about the destination of others? I would not wish an eternity in the lake of fire on my worst enemy. Would you wish it on your family and friends? Think about it.

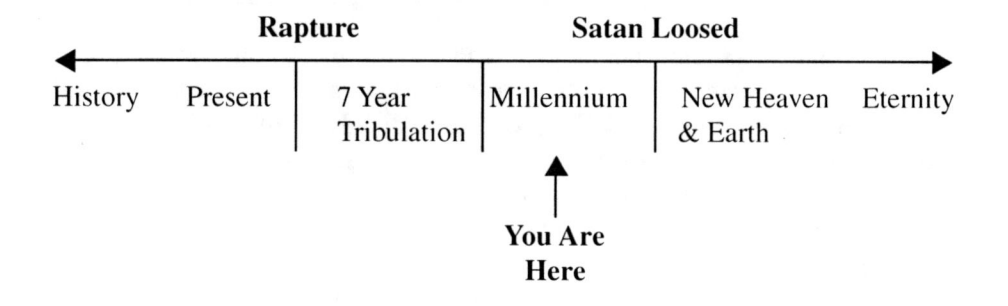

Not In A Thousand Years

	Rapture		Satan Loosed	
History	Present	7 Year Tribulation	Millennium	New Heaven & Earth	Eternity

↑
You Are Here

OLD TESTAMENT PASSAGES

Almost everyone affiliated with a church would agree that there is a heaven, and most would agree there is a hell. Now we turn our attention to a topic that is a little controversial. When you say the word millennium, some people might think Y2K. While the change in millennium brought some controversy, it was not as argumentative as the controversy over a future millennium the Bible describes. Millennium simply means a thousand-year period. And the Bible does speak of a future thousand-year period for earth. This period finds its roots in two Old Testament covenants, or contracts, and some prophecies. We will start our study by looking at these Old Testament passages, and then move on to some New Testament passages which shed some light on this future thousand year period of history. Finally, we will look at some of the different schools of thought about the millennium and compare them with what we have learned in our study of the scripture. Ready? Fasten your seatbelts, here we go.

> **READ:** GENESIS 15

The first contract is found in Genesis 15 and is called the Abrahamic Covenant. In verse one God identifies Himself to Abram. (Abram is Abraham before God changed his name in Genesis 17:5.) God identifies Himself as a protector of Abram, and the one who blessed Abram with his wealth. Abram was a wealthy person with much livestock and many servants.

Abram poses a question to God in verses two and three. "What is the point of blessing me with these riches if I have no son to inherit them?" Abram was seeing the blessings of God as useless because he had no one to pass them down to. He is expressing the oriental mindset of the importance of keeping your name alive through children, especially male children. Land and property were always passed to the children, specifically the male children. The firstborn son would always get the greatest share.

But, Abram had no children. He was in his eighties, and Sarai, his wife, was beyond childbearing years. So, Abram suggests that he should perform a common custom by adopting Eliezer, a child of one of the servants to be his heir. God would not hear of it. In verse four God is specific to Abram that the child would be his, not the product of someone else. God then takes Abram outside and has him try to count the stars. This was an illustration of how many descendants Abram would have. Even though he and his wife were old, Abram believed God. And God did fulfill this promise. Abram was the father of both Ishmael, the originator of the Arabs, and Isaac, the patriarch of the Jews.

Once the issue of descendants is cleared up, God begins to discuss a particular parcel of land. Abram wants some confirmation that he will gain possession of this land, and will be able to leave it as an inheritance. God's solution was simple. He simply made a contract with Abram.

It was a custom in the ancient oriental culture for two people to seal the deal, or make a contract, by performing a certain ritual. An animal would be sacrificed and split in two. The carcass would then be placed on two altars and the fires lit. The two men would walk between the altars as a confirmation to each other, before their god, that they would uphold their responsibility in the contract. Each man was pledging to be responsible for his part of the deal.

God had Abram get a heifer, a goat, a ram, and two birds for a sacrifice. According to the custom, Abram split the larger animals, and then placed a bird on each altar. There may have been multiple altars involved with this contract. All through the day Abram waited for God to come so that they could walk together between the sacrifices. He had to fend off the buzzards and other birds that wanted to eat the carcasses. Finally, at sunset, Abram fell into a deep sleep.

It is at this point that God came and told Abram what was going to happen to his family in Egypt. His family would be slaves in Egypt for four hundred years, but then they would return to the land promised to Abram. As the sun set, God walked between the sacrifices by Himself. Verse 17 describes God as a burning lamp, and a smoking furnace. By walking between the sacrifices by Himself, God was taking all of the responsibility for the fulfillment of the contract upon Himself. Abram had no responsibility, and did not need to take any action in order for the covenant to be completed. It was all on God.

This was an unconditional contract. No matter what Abram did or did not do, his descendants were going to inherit that land. The land would reach from the river of Egypt, which some think is a reference to the Nile, all the way to the Euphrates River, which runs through Iraq and Turkey. This is a huge territory that has never been completely claimed by the descendants of Abram.

There is also another interpretation to this land grant. There is a river called the River of Egypt that runs from the southern bend of the Mediterranean Sea toward the Sinai Peninsula. Abram would have been familiar with this river as his travels took him into that area. If that is the southern boundary of this land, then Solomon may have come close to holding the entire land grant from God. His kingdom extended from the River of Egypt in the south, to Syria in the north, with economic influence all the way north to the Euphrates. But, even with this interpretation, the descendants of Abram did not physically possess all of the land area granted by God in this covenant.

It is unclear what "River of Egypt" means. Scholars continue to debate it. Most would hold to one of the two theories mentioned, and by both theories, the descendants of Abram have yet to take full possession of the territory. This means that the fulfillment of this unconditional Abrahamic Covenant is still in the future.

Who Are The Descendants?

God is very clear when He establishes who the descendants are that will inherit the land promised to Abraham. In Genesis 15:2–4, Abraham thought that Eliezer, a servant born in his house, would be his heir. But God says that Eliezer is not going to be the one to inherit anything. It will be someone who is fathered by Abraham.

So, in chapter 16 of Genesis, Abraham and his wife Sarah try an old custom and have a child through his servant Hagar. The child's name is Ishmael. In the next chapter, Genesis 17:17–22, Abraham asks God if Ishmael will be the heir. But God flatly rejects this and declares that Isaac, a son who will be born to Sarah, will be the heir to the promised land.

Isaac then has a son named Jacob, who God will later rename Israel. In Genesis 28:13–15, God confirms His land contract with Jacob. He is now the heir to whom the land will be passed. It is the descendants of Jacob who spent 400 years in slavery in Egypt, and then returned to the land that was promised them. It is the nation of Israel that is clearly supposed to have control of the land promised by God.

READ: 2 SAMUEL 7:1–16

The second covenant, or contract, is called the Davidic Covenant. It is found in the passage we just looked at in 2 Samuel, and also in 1 Chronicles 17:1–14. It is a contract God made with David concerning his family's right to rule the kingdom of Israel.

The passage begins with David concerned over the fact that he is sitting in this fine palace, while the ark of God, the place where God's presence was made known, was in a flimsy tent. David loved God and wanted to show Him the utmost respect He deserved. He thought it was demeaning to God to have His sacred Ark of the Covenant in a simple tent. David wanted to build God a great temple with the finest wood and stones, and lots of gold and precious stones. But God did not allow David to build the temple.

God was not being mean to David by not allowing him to build this temple for Him. Actually, the blessing God gave him overshadowed the disappointment of not being allowed to build the temple. This is seen through the praise that David gives to God immediately following the passage in 2 Samuel. God promised David that instead of building a temple, a house for God, God would provide a house, a dynasty, for David. Remember that the perpetuation of a person's life through his heirs is very important in David's culture. This is especially true when you are talking about having a never-ending line of kings.

This contract, like the contract with Abram, is an unconditional contract, and has God as the sole person responsible in acting to fulfill it. Neither David, nor his heirs, can do anything to keep this contract in force, or to break it. It is all up to God.

So, what did God really promise David? He promised David that his heirs would always have a right to the throne of Israel, as long as there was a country and a king. Before David, a man named Saul had been king of Israel. Saul did not follow God and God took the kingdom from him and cut off his line from inheriting the throne ever again. God promised David that this would not happen to his descendants (2 Samuel 7:15). David's heirs would always have the right to the throne.

However, God did promise in verse 14 of the 2 Samuel passage that He would chasten, or punish, any of David's line who did not follow Him. The right to rule would never be taken away, but the kingdom could be overcome by outsiders. The kingdom, or country, of Israel has suffered such punishment several times. The country split into a Northern Kingdom and a Southern Kingdom soon after Solomon, David's son who built the temple, died. The two kingdoms were conquered by Assyria and Babylon respectively, thereby eliminating Israel as a country. Israel was allowed to return during the days of Cyrus, king of Persia, who conquered the Babylonians. But, they have not had a king on the throne since the original dispersion into Babylon. Even today, no king rules Israel.

The important parts of this Davidic Covenant are that, first, it is another unilateral, unconditional contract made by God. Second, it gives the right to rule as king over Israel only to the heirs of David. This is very important when it is coupled with the fact that the Abrahamic covenant has yet to be fulfilled. At some point in the future there will be a kingdom, or country, of Israel that covers the full land area promised by God to Abraham. If there is to be a king of this nation, then it will have to be an heir to David's throne. God would allow no one else.

> **READ:** ISAIAH 9:1–7

Just after David's son Solomon died, there was a civil war in Israel for control of the kingdom. The country split into the northern country, which continued to call itself Israel, and the southern country, which was called Judah. The heirs of David continued to rule over Judah from Jerusalem, while various people from Samaria ruled the northern country. In 722 B.C., Israel was conquered by the Assyrians. Judah was spared, and remained until 586 when they were taken into captivity by Babylon.

Isaiah was a prophet in Judah between 740 and 680 B.C. This was the time when the turbulent overthrow of the Northern Kingdom occurred. God showed Isaiah that the same thing was going to happen to Judah, if things did not change. While many of Isaiah's prophecies are of destruction, some of them were of restoration. Isaiah 9:1–7 is one such prophecy.

Matthew quotes the first part of this prophecy as applying to Jesus during His teaching ministry in Galilee. It is the last part, verses 6 and 7 which we need to really examine. Here God is promising a King that would rise up to rule Israel. This King would have specific qualities. Almost everyone agrees that this is a prophecy about the coming Christ or Messiah, whom we hold to be Jesus. In fact, this verse is often used in sermons around Christmas time to show the foretelling of Jesus' birth. No other king of Israel after Isaiah's time, or even before, had these particular qualities.

First, the government will be on His shoulder. The Hebrew has it in the present tense; "the government is on His shoulder." While the rulers of Israel were constantly on His back, the government was never on Jesus' shoulder. He never had to bear the responsibility of government while He was here on earth. Yet, because of the wording, it is a certainty that this will happen. At some point the Messiah will bear the responsibility of government.

Second, He has many descriptive names. Any king would have the responsibility of government, but it is the names given to this particular king that make Him unique and show us that it is Jesus the Messiah Who is being described. The most striking name is "The mighty God." This would be blasphemy, a sin against God where a person lies about God, if the person on the throne were not God Himself. God states that this person is going to be called the mighty God, and the everlasting Father. These are names used only for God, and yet,

God is all right with this person being called God. The only person Who could hold this title, and Who has walked this earth, is Jesus. He was God walking around in flesh.

Third, this King will sit on the throne of David and rule his kingdom. There is nothing in the text that suggests that this is a spiritual kingdom, and will only be realized in heaven. Everything has been in physical reality. The earlier prophecy of Jesus being in Galilee was physical, not spiritual. The prophecy about Jesus going to sit on the throne of David, and rule over David's kingdom, is physical reality, not spiritual. Jesus did not fulfill this when He was here the first time. Therefore, at some point, this has to be fulfilled, or God is a liar. Hopefully we all know that God always tells the truth.

The interesting thing about this prophecy is that it is another unilateral statement. There are no "if then" clauses. If Judah will do this, then God will do that, is not found. The final words of verse seven tell us that it is God Himself who will do this. Judah and Israel have no responsibility or act to perform in order to bring this prophecy about. There is nothing that they could do to stop it from happening either. Their rejection of Jesus the first time did not thwart God's plan or promise in this matter. They could do nothing to stop this from happening.

From this prophecy we have found out that Jesus is to be the King of Israel and sit on David's throne, ruling David's kingdom. This event will be physical in nature, not spiritual, and it cannot be thwarted by any action of man because God is the one Who will do it. This event has not yet happened.

READ: ISAIAH 11:1–11

Isaiah begins this part of his prophecy talking about a rod coming from a stump and a branch from a root. What is he talking about? Well, what verse one tells us is that the kings of Judah are going to be cut off (like a stump). Remember, the kings of Judah were descendants of David. Isaiah is saying that these kings are not going to be able to rule over Judah any more because it will be destroyed.

In 586, the Babylonians swept into Judah and took Jerusalem. They took captives back to Babylon, including the king and his household. The rule of these kings was ended, and still to this day has not been reestablished. Yet, the bloodline of David is still intact.

This prophecy says that a King (a branch or rod) will rise from this family of kings to take the throne once again. Almost everyone agrees that this prophecy is talking about Jesus. Just like the prophecy we just looked at in chapter nine, the description of this King could only fit Jesus. No human could measure up to the standards set by this description.

Verse six begins the description of this King's kingdom or rule. It describes a period of absolute peace, even among the animals. This King will be from Jesse, who was David's father. Even people who are not Jewish (Gentiles) will look to this King and seek Him out.

One of the key verses is verse eleven. It talks about the Jewish people being recovered from dispersion all over the earth for the second time. What is so striking about this passage is that it is said before it was even necessary for the first reunion. The southern kingdom of Judah had not yet fallen to Babylon. At least half the kingdom was still intact. The first gathering did not occur until after Judah fell and spent seventy years in captivity. This was after the writing of this prophecy. And yet, Isaiah is talking about a second recovery of the Jewish nation to the land where they belong.

This prophecy is still future. Like the other prophecy it cannot be spiritualized. There are too many specific details that have to take place in this physical realm, such as the reuniting of Israel under this king, and gathering of the gentiles, for this to be spiritual in nature. And, it is generally conceded that Jesus is the One Who is spoken of in this passage. Yet, He did not accomplish this when He was here the first time. There is nothing in this passage that says that people rejecting this King could thwart this plan. The way it is written, it is a definite event in future history.

SUMMARY OF OLD TESTAMENT PASSAGES

Lets us take just a minute and review what we have learned from these passages in the Old Testament. Then, we will move on to some passages in the New Testament and see what they have to say.

- ♦ We learned that the contract God made with Abram (the Abrahamic Covenant) was a land grant of considerable size. It was a land grant which Abram's heirs would inherit from God. This contract has not been fully realized yet and still remains a future event.

- ♦ The contract God made with David was for his heirs to always have the right to the throne of Israel. This is still true, even today.

- ♦ Both contracts were unilateral. The only person Who had any responsibility, or had to perform any action, for these contracts to be fulfilled was God. There was nothing that anyone could do to stop these contracts from being fulfilled.

- Isaiah taught us that there was going to be a future King of Israel Who would be God Himself, ruling on the throne of David, and over the restored kingdom of David. These prophecies relate to physical events, and are dependent solely on God to perform. There is nothing anyone can do to keep these events from happening.

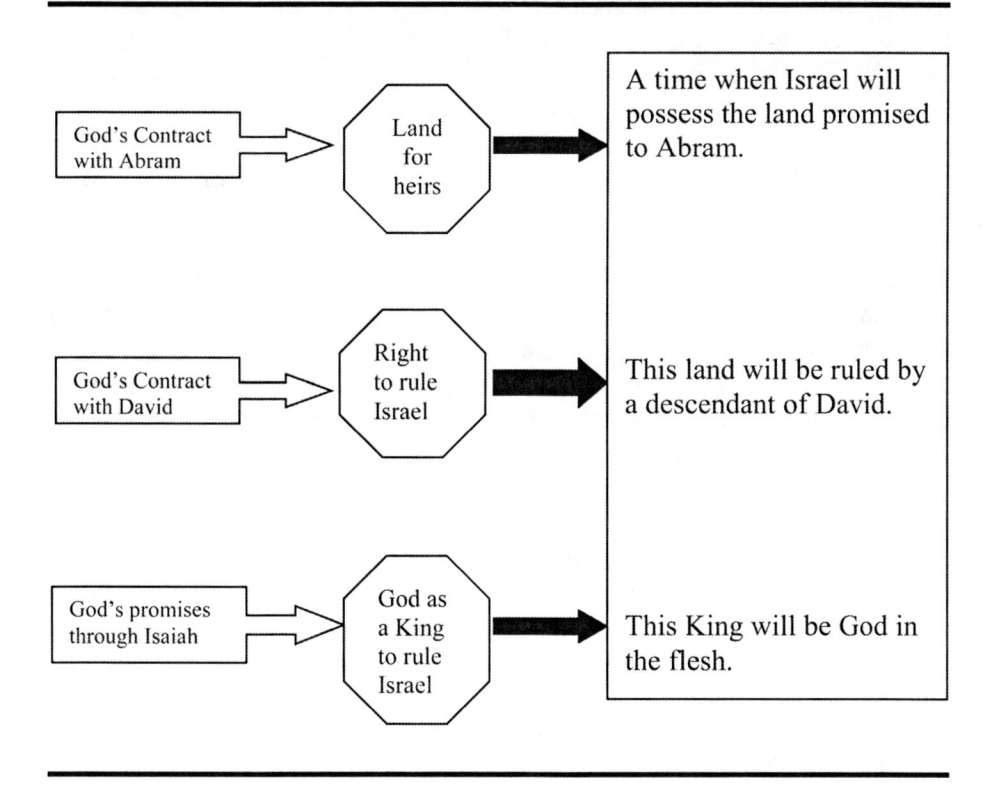

God's Contract with Abram	Land for heirs	A time when Israel will possess the land promised to Abram.
God's Contract with David	Right to rule Israel	This land will be ruled by a descendant of David.
God's promises through Isaiah	God as a King to rule Israel	This King will be God in the flesh.

NEW TESTAMENT PASSAGES

> **READ:** EITHER MATTHEW 1:1–17 OR LUKE 3:23–38

As we studied the Old Testament passages, we noted that the prophecies of Isaiah were widely accepted as referring to Jesus. But, is this true? Does Jesus have the right to the throne of David? Is He an heir of David? The gospel writers Matthew and Luke both answer this question. Both give the genealogy of Jesus. However, their lists of relatives do not match. There is a good reason for this.

Matthew draws his genealogy of Jesus from Joseph's family line. Joseph was the husband of Mary, but not the physical father of Jesus. God was the Father of Jesus through Mary who was a virgin. Yet, the lineage of Joseph is important because he could still hand down the right to the throne. Also, some who did not believe in the virgin birth could have questioned Jesus' right to the throne if Joseph was not a descendant of David.

The Christmas story would not have been the same if Joseph had not been a descendant of David. The taxation ordered by the Roman government required that people return to their town of family origin. The town of David's family was Bethlehem. That is where Jesus was supposed to be born according to the prophecy (Micah 5:2).

Joseph's line is taken through Solomon, the son of David who took the throne after David and built the temple. As we go down the list of ancestors we come to the name Jechonias (11). This is Jechoniah, (also known as Jehoiachin) the last king of Judah before it fell to Babylon. Jeremiah gave this king a nickname of Coniah. Apparently the prophet did not have much respect for this particular king to give him a nickname. This king only ruled for three months before being carted away as a prisoner to Babylon.

Jehoiachin, Coniah, was cursed by God (Jeremiah 22:30). Neither he, nor any of his descendants, would have a profitable rule on the throne of David. God did not cut them off from ruling, but He would never allow them to be prosperous on the throne. Because Jesus was not the physical son of Joseph, He missed this curse of the bloodline. Had He not missed this curse, Jesus would never be able to fulfill the prophecies concerning a future prosperous King ruling over the full extent of the land of Israel promised to Abraham.

Luke takes his genealogy from Mary. The two lines diverge at David's sons (31). Joseph's line was through Solomon, while Mary's line was through Nathan, a half brother to Solomon (2 Samuel 5:13, 14). The true bloodline of

Jesus was through Mary as she was the physical mother of Jesus. It is through Mary that Jesus has the true right to the throne of David, and avoids the curse that had befallen Joseph's line.

Both genealogies show Jesus to be a descendant of Abraham, which is important. Only a descendant of Abraham could take part in the land grant that was promised to Abraham's descendants. Luke takes his genealogy all the way back to Adam. He decided to go from Son of God to son of God. Matthew considers it enough to show the line to Abraham.

These genealogies prove that, no matter how you cut it, Jesus was and is entitled to the throne of David. He is the Son of God, God Himself, Who can rule over the land promised to Abraham. Jesus alone can fulfill the prophecies we studied in Isaiah. Not only is He God, but He is the living firstborn Son in the line of David, and therefore would have precedent over anyone else who might claim the right to the throne today. Jesus will have to be the next true King of Israel; all others would be usurpers to the throne.

READ: LUKE 24:13–48 and ACTS 1:6–11

According to the scriptures we just read, Jesus went through all the Old Testament scriptures about Himself twice. The first time He was on a road walking toward Emmaus with two disciples who did not know Who He was. The second time was with these disciples and at least ten of the other disciples. We do not know if Thomas was present during this meeting. Jesus did not just list the scriptures; He opened up their understanding about the scriptures. He gave them the correct interpretation of the prophecies about Himself.

Jesus needed to accomplish at least two things by holding this Bible study. First, He needed to show the disciples that the Messiah had to die to pay for the sin of the world. Second, He needed to clarify the scriptures about the coming kingdom that would be ruled by this Messiah, or Christ.

At the time of Jesus, every person with Jewish blood in them was looking for the Messiah to come and save them from the Roman occupation. They understood that this King would set up a revived kingdom of Israel that would be even better than the kingdom David ruled over. They ignored the prophecies about the suffering Messiah who would die for the sin of the world. It could be that this was not taught by the religious leaders of that time. This prospect of a kingdom was what the disciples expected.

The Messiah, according to the tradition of the time, would never die. He would set up His kingdom forever. That is one reason why the crucifixion and burial of Jesus was so devastating to the disciples. Their Messiah had died. Their hopes for the kingdom died with it.

Jesus opened up their minds to the truth, that He died to pay the price for sin. This was the spiritual aspect of the Messiah. He had paid for the soul/spirit of every person who would ever live on earth, so that they could be a part of the eternal physical/spiritual kingdom of heaven.

Then, Jesus turned His attention to passages like the Isaiah passages we studied. He told the disciples the truth about the kingdom here on earth. He did not want them to have any misconceptions about His setting up an earthly kingdom for a restored Israel.

Now, with that in mind, we need to look at the passage in Acts. Jesus had led the disciples up to the Mount of Olives, a place that was prominent in the final week of Jesus. While they are there the disciples ask Jesus if He is going to set up the kingdom of Israel now. They were looking for a physical kingdom to be established on earth. Jesus did not rebuke them. He did not ask them if they had been listening during His previous teaching. He simply says it is not yet time, and it is not for them to know the time. In other words, there is going to be a physical kingdom of Israel at some point in the future, just not right at that time.

Jesus goes on to point the disciples to the more important task of building the spiritual kingdom of God by spreading the gospel. It is more important that people's eternal destinies be assured than to have a temporary, physical kingdom established for Israel.

This was a last chance to set the disciples straight, if there was not going to be a physical kingdom on earth for Israel. But, Jesus never said that there would not be a physical kingdom, in fact He states there is a time when it is coming. He does establish that the soul/spirit of people is more important, and a higher priority on God's list.

As soon as Jesus finished saying this, He ascends up into the clouds. The disciples stand there gawking up at the sky where He went, and two angels stand with them. The angels asked them why they were standing there. They had their orders, get going. Jesus was going to return just as He left, physically. The disciples needed to get people ready for the eternal state by spreading the gospel. When God decided it was time, Jesus would return. But, until then, keep working at God's plan for man.

> **READ:** REVELATION 20:1–10

Perhaps you noticed as you read this passage that a thousand years kept coming up. It is from this passage that we get the time frame for the kingdom Jesus will rule on earth. Let us just go through the passage and see how the events unfold.

The time of verse one is directly following the battle of Armageddon, which we will discuss in a later chapter. Satan has been wreaking havoc on the earth, especially the last seven years, and God has now put an end to his reign. God sends an angel with a great, supernatural chain to bind Satan and throw him into the bottomless pit. This is a reference to hell, the temporary holding place for the soul/spirit of refusers. Satan is to be bound for 1,000 years, a millennium. He will not be able to deceive anyone on earth during this time. But, he will be turned loose after 1,000 years is over, at least for a little time.

Starting in verse four we see a group of people who are unfamiliar to us right now because we have yet to study them. For the past seven years on earth, previous to the time of this passage, there had been a great tribulation on the earth. Satan had ruled the earth with his person in charge of a one-world government. During this time there were some who accepted Jesus into their lives. These people were hated by the government and put to death. Apparently they were beheaded. The government had required a mark of loyalty, and for them to worship the Beast, the leader of the government. These people would not accept the mark or worship the Beast, and they paid for it with their lives. They stayed true to Jesus.

These people are now resurrected. Their soul/spirit is retrieved from heaven and their bodies from the earth, and joined together. Jesus sets up a kingdom for 1,000 years where He is the ruler of the earth. These resurrected accepters reign with Jesus for 1,000 years on the earth. But everyone else who is dead is not resurrected until after the 1,000 years is over.

But, after 1,000 years, Satan is set loose to tempt people and deceive them. We wonder why God would allow Satan to be loosed? Some people will be born during this thousand-year reign of Jesus. They will have never had the chance to see both sides of the coin and choose to follow God over the temptation of Satan. God wants us to truly love Him, and that kind of love can only come by choice. Even after living all their lives under the authority of Jesus with all the peace and love, Satan will actually be able to find a great many people who choose to refuse to give Jesus a place in their life. Satan will have enough followers to form a huge army to surround Jerusalem. But God sends fire down from heaven and destroys them. Satan is then cast into the lake of fire to spend eternity with his henchmen, the beast and false prophet.

These events form a consecutive timeline. There are no breaks or interruptions. There is also no logical way to shuffle the events into a different order. Because the events are all closely linked, especially in reference to time, they must all either be interpreted as physically happening, or as just a picture with some spiritual meaning.

Could this be interpreted as just a spiritual allegory? In order to interpret this as just a story with a spiritual lesson, we would have to assume that none of the characters or events or places is real. The time of 1,000 years is merely symbolic, as is the binding of Satan and his subsequent release. The resurrection of the martyrs, their reign with Jesus, and the rebellion by the refusers, are simply symbols of a deep spiritual truth, and will not really happen. The lake of fire is nothing more than an illustration, and little better than a myth. This kind of interpretation does violence to other content in the Bible, and especially this passage.

This passage must be interpreted at face value. When it says Satan is confined in hell for 1,000 years and then released, it means just that. When it says that tribulation martyrs ruled with Jesus on earth for 1,000 years, it means just that. When it says that there was a rebellion by those who refused God, it means just that. And, when it says that Satan is cast into the lake of fire, it means just that. There is no deeper, hidden, spiritual meaning. John, the writer, is relating events as he sees them happen.

SUMMARY OF NEW TESTAMENT PASSAGES

- Jesus is of the line of David and, therefore, has the right to take the throne of a restored kingdom of Israel. He is the eldest firstborn, which places Him above anyone else in line for the throne.

- Before His ascension into heaven, Jesus told the disciples everything the Old Testament had to say about Him. This included the passages concerning the coming kingdom and His rule over it. He never corrected the disciples in their belief that there was going to be a physical kingdom set up on earth, He merely told them that the time was not yet here. He wanted their emphasis to be on building the kingdom of God by winning the souls of men, instead of working to build the infrastructure for a new kingdom of Israel.

- Satan is going to be bound for 1,000 years. During this time Jesus is going to reign on the earth. When the 1,000 years is over, there will be a time for Satan to deceive people one more time. He will gather a vast army against Jesus, but God will destroy them with fire. Satan will be cast into the lake of fire to spend eternity.

SUMMARY OF BIBLE PASSAGES

Now it is time for us to put all these passages together and see what we have learned.

- God made a contract with Abram that has yet to be fulfilled. This contract was totally dependent on God to fulfill. Neither Abram, nor his heirs could break the contract in any way, or cause God to not fulfill it.
- God made a contract with David that his heirs would always be on the throne of Israel when they have a king. If a new kingdom comprised of the land promised to Abram is established, then the rightful king will have to be a descendant of David.
- Isaiah foretold of a future kingdom of Israel ruled by an heir of David, Who is also God.
- Jesus is an heir of David through His biological mother, Mary, and His adoptive father, Joseph. Because of the resurrection, Jesus is still alive, making Him the oldest Son, and firstborn, to inherit the throne when it becomes available. No one else has the right to that throne until Jesus abdicates.
- Jesus never discouraged the disciples in their belief of a physical kingdom of Israel yet to come, with Him as its King.
- According to the book of Revelation, there is going to be a thousand-year period when Satan is bound and Jesus rules on the earth. After this is a period of rebellion, led by the released Satan, which is put down by God destroying the refusers. Satan ends up in the lake of fire for eternity.

THREE SCHOOLS OF THOUGHT

There are three schools of thought about this 1,000-year period mentioned in Revelation 20. Using the word millennium as its base, the schools of thought put their prefixes to the word millennialism. We will look at each school individually, and compare their teachings with what we have just learned from our study of scripture.

> ## AMILLENNIALISM
>
> ### A (No) + Millennium = No millennium
>
> This school of thought says that there is no future, physical millennial reign of Christ on earth. It sees the promise of a kingdom being fulfilled in a "spiritual kingdom" which is now present.

This school spiritualizes any prophecies that reference a future kingdom. To them, Isaiah's prophecies are talking about a spiritual kingdom that Jesus rules over today from heaven. Jesus, according to them, never spoke of the future kingdom on earth, only the kingdom of heaven. They would consider the church as the kingdom on earth that Jesus rules from heaven. Eventually everything will end and accepters will end up with Jesus in heaven.

This school discounts the book of Revelation, as a whole. They hold that John was just talking about events in his time, or, at best, writing a spiritual allegory for believers of all ages. They would never consider any of the events to be real, or take place in the future, physical world.

So, how does this school stack up to the few scriptures we studied? The contract with Abram is left unfulfilled. God does not keep His promise. Israel never gains the full territory God promised to them. This makes God a liar, which we know He is not.

The contract with David could be considered covered because one of his heirs was always on the throne when there was a king. With this school of thought there will never be another king in Israel, and no need for an heir of David.

The prophecies of Isaiah are null and void. This school teaches that the Jews voided the contract with God when they rejected Jesus as their King during His time on earth. However, as we studied, these promises were to be carried out by God alone, and were unconditional. Neither the Jews nor the Gentiles could do anything to stop these prophecies from being fulfilled. Remember in Isaiah 11:10 that Gentiles, non-Jews, are mentioned as seeking this King. That was not made void by the Romans' actions in crucifying Jesus. Only God could void these prophecies, and He gave no conditions under which they might be voided.

According to this school of thought, Jesus lied to His disciples. He did not tell them the truth that there is no kingdom of Israel coming because the Jews rejected Him and crucified Him. Even after His resurrection, just before He returned to heaven, Jesus allowed the disciples to believe in the coming physical kingdom. He did try to keep their focus on the Kingdom of God, the higher priority, but He only said that it was not yet time for the physical kingdom. Jesus was simply saying that it is up to us to lead people into the kingdom of God; it is God's responsibility to set up the physical kingdom on earth. We are to preach the way to the kingdom of God, not the way to the physical kingdom on earth.

This school completely discounts the scripture in Revelation concerning the 1,000 years.

This school leads to an inconsistent and dangerous interpretation of scripture. In order to maintain the structure of this system, scripture has to be twisted or dismissed. It is inconsistent to make the prophecies about Jesus' first coming, (the birth in Bethlehem, born of a virgin, the suffering on the cross), literal and physical in interpretation, and yet make the scripture about His ruling a future kingdom simply spiritual.

Interpretation of this type can lead to some severe doctrinal errors. First, it says that God can lie, which would make Him unholy. Holiness is at the root of God's being. Second, it would have to deny the existence of eternal punishment in the lake of fire, since Revelation is the book that gives us this doctrine. At the same time, you would have to do away with the new heaven and earth. Third, if there was consistency in their interpretation, the virgin birth would be just a spiritual picture, along with the cross. Neither would be real, physical events.

The system of interpretation used by this school does damage to the scriptures. The Bible is not interpreted with integrity and honesty, but twisted to what the individual wants it to mean in order to uphold the system he has concocted.

| CURRENT AGE | JESUS RETURNS FOR ETERNAL STATE |

> ## POST-MILLENNIALISM
>
> ### Post (After) + Millennium = After the millennium
>
> This school believes in a more or less literal millennium (which they consider a golden age) in the future, which results from the spread of the gospel over the earth. Jesus is seen as returning to earth at the close of this period.

The time sequence for this school would look something like this. At some point in the future Satan is going to be bound. His influence will no longer affect the earth. This will last for a thousand years. During this time the gospel will spread throughout the world bringing about a Christian world of peace and prosperity. After these thousand years is finished, Jesus will return to earth to set up the eternal state.

This school has the same problem with the contracts made by God to Abram and David as the amillennialist school. The Abrahamic Covenant is broken and unfulfilled. Israel does not inherit the land promised to them. The promises made through Isaiah are left unfulfilled. There is no kingdom of Israel to rule.

To this school's credit, they do recognize the fact that Jesus placed an emphasis on preparing people for the eternal kingdom of God instead of the temporary kingdom on earth. But they miss the fact that Jesus did not discount the physical kingdom, with Him as its King. It seems that this school has the right priorities, the preaching of the gospel, but the wrong interpretation of some scripture in forming their ideas of future events.

The passage in Revelation 20 is accounted for, but not completely. This school sees the binding of Satan, but misses his being set free to deceive people for one last time after the thousand years. They have us going from this golden age straight into eternity. There is no gap there to accommodate Satan's return and the final battle where God destroys the refusers.

Apparently this school has some of the same problems with the scriptures as the previous school. But, it also poses some new problems. This school fails to recognize the truth, that man is getting worse, not better. Even left to our own devices, without Satan's influence, we are still sinners and refusers of God. This school lays all of the responsibility on man to bring about the kingdom on earth. But, God is the one Who will create the kingdom as He promised. Man could never create a utopian Christian environment that is described in Isaiah 11.

This school has some good points. Their focus on the gospel, and their acknowledgment of the eternal state for both refusers and accepters is great. But, there are gaps and problems with their interpretation and understanding of the scripture. They seem to put more emphasis on man accomplishing something, when it is really up to God to fulfill His promises.

| CURRENT AGE | 1,000 YEAR "GOLDEN AGE" | JESUS RETURNS FOR ETERNAL STATE |

> ### PREMILLENNIALISM
>
> **Pre (Before) + Millennium = Before the Millennium**
>
> This school believes that Jesus returns to earth to set up a literal, physical kingdom of Israel from which Jesus will rule the earth for 1,000 years.

The time sequence for this school follows the pattern of Revelation 20. Jesus returns to earth to destroy Satan and his armies at the Battle of Armageddon (which we have not yet talked about). Following the battle, Satan is bound in the bottomless pit and Jesus sets up His kingdom. Israel, as one of the nations in the world, receives all the territory promised to Abram. Jesus rules the world from Israel, which fulfills the Davidic Covenant. This kingdom will last for a thousand years, at which time, Satan will be loosed for an undisclosed amount of time to gather a new army against Jesus. God destroys this army and Satan is condemned to the lake of fire for eternity. Then comes the eternal state with the new heaven and earth and the lake of fire.

All of the covenants made by God to Israel are taken into account with this school's sequence of events. The land is given to Israel, and the heir of David, who is God, reigns on its throne. All of the prophecies of Isaiah are covered. God does rule, and there is a time of absolute peace for a thousand years. Jesus' comment to His disciples about it not yet being time is not damaged. And the passage in Revelation holds its full integrity with no twisting. This is the best fit for the Bible passages we have studied.

Those who hold to this school of thought are strong in the area of evangelism. They realize that the emphasis of Jesus was on the eternal kingdom of God, yet they do not discount the coming physical kingdom. They also realize that the teaching about the lake of fire is just as serious as the teaching of the new heaven and earth. It is the eternal state of people that is most important. The Millennium is simply another temporary step to that eternal end.

| Jesus returns/ Satan is bound | 1,000 year reign of Jesus on earth | Satan loosed | Final Rebellion | White Throne | Eternal State |

SUMMARY OF THE THREE SCHOOLS

The amillennial and postmillennial schools have severe problems with proper interpretation of the scriptures. In some instances their integrity is lost as they twist meanings and ignore passages and books. The premillennial school takes into account all scriptures without damage to the integrity of any passage or book, and seems to fit the scriptures better than the other two.

POPULATION

READ: MATTHEW 25:31–46

There is one final subject we need to look at before leaving the topic of the millennium. Who is going to populate this kingdom? One thing is for certain; the population will be made up of those who are alive. That sounds appropriately vague, so let me try to explain.

We have to remember that when Jesus returns to set up the kingdom, the earth will have been suffering through seven years of tribulation. (We will begin discussing this in the next chapter.) Many people during this seven years will accept Jesus, many will not. When the armies of the earth are wiped out by Jesus at Armageddon, there will still be people who are alive on the earth. Jesus tells us in Matthew about the sorting out of those who are alive on the earth at this time. This sorting is called the Judgment of the Nations. (I will sometimes refer to this as the sheep and goat judgment.)

Those who have accepted Jesus into their life, the sheep, will show this by their actions during the tribulation. They will be kind toward other accepters, helping them survive the cruel world government. Those who have refused Jesus, the goats, will demonstrate this by their actions of persecuting the accepters. The accepters will enter into the kingdom alive, but the refusers will be placed in hell to await their judgment before the great white throne.

We have already looked at Revelation 20 and seen that there will be some accepters who do not make it through the tribulation period. The government will have martyred them. These people will be resurrected to rule in the kingdom with Jesus.

Daniel 12:1–3 tells us that right after the tribulation period, but before the kingdom begins, there will be a resurrection of the Old Testament saints. Like the tribulation saints, they will have their soul/spirit reunited with their bodies in order to live within the kingdom. The promise of possessing the land and having a kingdom was to the Old Testament people. Those who believed in God, and allowed Him into their lives deserve to enter into this kingdom they looked for, and wanted. God is faithful in keeping His promises. Those of that time who did not accept God into their lives will remain in the temporary holding place for the refusers until the lake of fire is ready for them.

These three groups will enter the kingdom and be bound for an eternity in the new heaven and earth when it is over. But there will be others in the kingdom. My speculation is that there will be no death during this time, or maybe there will be. The only reason I could see for someone dying would be his or her blatant refusal to follow Jesus. But, this will not happen until Satan is released after the thousand years is over. So, I do not see anyone dying, and everyone living at least until the thousand years are over. Those who enter the kingdom alive because they have accepted Jesus and lived through the tribulation period will have children during these thousand years. These children will be the ones that Satan tempts when he is released. Those who refuse Jesus end up in hell, and those who accept Jesus enter into the eternal state without dying.

To sum up, there is going to be a population who inhabits the kingdom with resurrected bodies: the Old Testament saints, and the tribulation saints. There will be those who are in the kingdom with their natural bodies: those accepters who made it through the tribulation alive, and their children born in the kingdom. (There may also be children who enter the kingdom from the tribulation period.) Those accepters who are in their natural bodies at the end of the kingdom will have their bodies changed before entering the new heaven and earth.

OVERALL SUMMARY

We have seen from scripture that there is coming a time when Jesus will return to earth to take the throne of the restored kingdom of Israel. This kingdom will contain all the land that was promised by God to Abraham's descendants. It will be ruled by a descendant of David, fulfilling God's promise to him. This king will be God, Jesus, fulfilling the prophecies of Isaiah. The kingdom will have a thousand years of peace while Satan is bound.

It will be populated by those accepters from the Old Testament and tribulation period who have been resurrected, along with accepters who survived the tribulation period, and their children. When Satan is released, these children will have to decide whom to follow. Many will follow Satan and be destroyed.

After this kingdom comes the eternal state of a new heaven and earth, and the lake of fire.

MIND THE GAP

As we study the Millennium we realize that God does fulfill His promises. He has integrity. To the Old Testament saints He promised a kingdom where they could take part. These people are resurrected to take their place in this earthly kingdom. Israel finally has the land and the King that was promised to them.

I can see how God kept His promises to those in the Old Testament. Abraham received a son, and David received a permanent grant to his family being on the throne. And, I can see how God is planning on fulfilling the rest of His promises. That gives me encouragement for today.

When Jesus said that He would always be with me (Matthew 28:20), I know that He will keep that promise. This means that He is with me today, right now. Jesus also said that, if I believe in Him, I will have eternal life (John 3:16). I can take that promise to the bank also.

While the kingdom is important to God in that He keeps His promises and upholds His integrity, it is far more important to God that we share the truth about Him with others. It is more important to God that we spend an eternity with Him in heaven, than enter into the thousand years of His perfect kingdom. Jesus' final words to His disciples, recorded in Matthew 28:18–20 and Acts 1:8, were words of command to go tell others the truth. He did not command them to tell about the kingdom, but about Him, and what He had done so that people might have a relationship with God.

This point is so important to God that, at the end of the millennium, He gives people one more chance to accept Him instead of following Satan. If spreading the truth is this important to God, what should we be doing about it?

The Tribulation Players

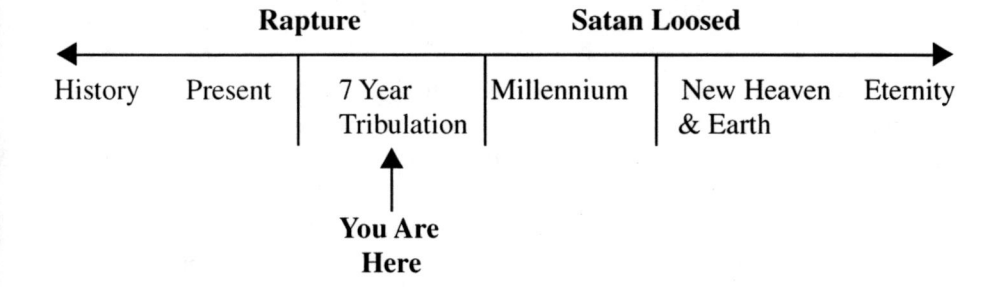

| History | Present | **Rapture**
 7 Year
 Tribulation | Millennium | **Satan Loosed**
 New Heaven
 & Earth | Eternity |

↑
You Are
Here

> READ: DANIEL 9:24–27

"All the world is a stage" is a very true statement when it comes to the next period of future history we are going to study. The time called the tribulation is the period most people usually focus their attention on when studying future events. This is probably because we have the most details about this short period. Most of the book of Revelation is taken up by covering these events. Jesus had a whole sermon recorded that gave the framework for this period. The prophet Daniel speaks of this time, as do other Old Testament prophets.

Tribulation	Millennial Kingdom	Eternity

Compared to the thousand years of the Millennial Kingdom of Jesus on earth that we just studied, the time period of the tribulation is very short, only seven years. We derive this figure from several sources, but especially from Daniel 9:24–27. In this passage God lays out His plan to Daniel for the reconciliation of Israel to God. The plan entails seventy weeks of years, or 490 years. Some dispute that this is actually years, but there is no way that the events can fit within an actual seventy weeks.

Daniel says that from the time a decree goes out to rebuild Jerusalem, it would take seven weeks and sixty-two weeks, for Messiah to appear on the scene. We know that Daniel lived during the captivity of Israel in Babylon. He was looking forward to a time when the people of Israel could return to Jerusalem, and their homeland. The Babylonians were conquered by the Persians. It is under the Persian rule that the Jews were allowed to return to their homeland, and begin rebuilding the city of Jerusalem.

This return and rebuilding took place somewhere between 440 and 500 B.C., which would begin the time line for Daniel's prophecy. We know that Jesus was not born until around 3 B.C., and His ministry lasted until about 30 A.D., at which time He was crucified (cut off). If Daniel was talking strictly weeks, then Jesus should have appeared on the scene approximately a year and a half after Jerusalem began to be rebuilt. But, He did not.

Daniel also speaks of those who destroy Jerusalem. He calls them the people of the coming prince. The coming prince is Anti-Christ. As we shall see later, he comes from the Roman people. The Romans do not destroy Jerusalem until 70 A.D., after the 69 weeks is over, but before the 70th week begins.

Another reason for believing that one week equals seven years in this passage, is because of verse 27. We will cover this more in depth later, but for now, a thumbnail sketch will do. This prince will make a contract with the people of Israel for one week. In the middle of that week, he will break the contract and desecrate the temple in Jerusalem, setting himself up to be god. Daniel 12:11 states that, from the time this desecration occurs, until the time of the end will be one thousand two hundred and ninety days. Other passages bear out that these really are days. That means that from the mid-point of the week, where Anti-Christ breaks his treaty, to the end, is approximately 3 ½ years. This would make the total week seven years.

Because the destruction of Jerusalem comes "after" the 69th week, it is held that there is a gap between the 69th and 70th week. Sixty-nine weeks have been completed. We are waiting for the seventieth. The seventieth week, which is seven years, is when we place the tribulation period we will be discussing. This is a time of terrible trouble and judgment on the earth.

7 WEEKS	62 WEEKS	GAP	1 WEEK
(49 Years)	(434 Years)	(Unknown Years)	(7 Years)
Rebuilding Jerusalem	To Messiah	Jerusalem destroyed	Tribulation Period

We will look at the tribulation in two sections. If you think of this as a play, we will be looking at the players, or characters, first. Then, in the next chapter, we will look at the plot, or sequence of events. We will start by dividing the characters into two sections. We will look at the unholy trinity (the bad guys), and then look at the good guys (the two Witnesses, the 144,000, and the Great Multitude).

THE DRAGON: SATAN

READ: REVELATION 12

The Apostle John, as part of his vision of future events given to him by God, sees this woman and a dragon. He identifies the Dragon in verse 9 as being Satan, the Devil. Knowing this helps us to interpret this passage a little easier.

We can figure out who the woman is if we know Who the Child is Whom she bore. Verse 5 states that this Child was "to rule all nations with a rod of iron." This is a description of Jesus the Messiah. The woman then is not Mary, but Israel. The events related in the passage take longer than Mary's lifetime to fulfill, and there is a sense that the woman represents something larger than a single person. The twelve stars may represent the original twelve sons of Jacob (Israel), who became the twelve tribes of Israel.

Now that we know who the key players are, let us take a look at what this passage is relating. Verses 1–4 give us the history of Israel and Satan prior to the birth of Jesus. God had promised that the Savior would come through Israel. Remember, He had to be of the line of David, a Son of Abraham. Satan knew this, and he tried everything he could think of to destroy Israel before this child was born. He turned Israel away from God by getting them to worship false gods. He tried to destroy them with other countries. God, Himself, sent them away to Assyria and Babylon because they rejected Him. But Israel was never wiped out. Verse 4 says that Satan cast a third of the stars to earth with his tail. Most people hold this to be a reference to the first rebellion by Satan against God. They believe that one-third of the angels (stars) followed Satan in this rebellion, and they were cast to the earth to work for him.

Satan knew that the time was coming when Jesus would enter this earth. Maybe he had someone tail Gabriel who gave the message to Mary and Joseph. At any rate he was ready. Or, at least he thought he was. Satan was behind the killing of the innocents by Herod. When Herod found out that a king was born in Bethlehem, he had all the male children under two years old killed. Jesus and his family fled to Egypt. All through His life Satan tried to tempt Jesus into sinning, or kill Him before His time. Everything Satan tried failed, even the crucifixion. Upon being raised from the dead, Jesus ascended back to heaven.

Between verses 5 and 6 are thousands of years. Verse 6 begins to relate the events of the tribulation period, but then sidesteps just a little to show what has taken place in heaven to bring about these events. Verse 6 really needs to be understood in connection with verse 14. They are speaking of the same event. During the last half of the tribulation [1,260 days; time, times, and half a time] Satan will persecute Israel more than she has ever been persecuted before. The reason for this persecution is spite.

Satan and his angels make a final attempt at overpowering the throne in heaven. Michael and his angels are in a war versus Satan and his angels. Satan loses and he and his henchmen are cast out of heaven for good and sent to the earth. Apparently Satan still has access to the throne of God up until this point. He accuses people before God, even Christians. But, the accusations stop when he is thrown out of heaven. Satan can no longer exert any influence in heaven. So, he takes it out on the earth, specifically the people of God.

We do not know exactly when this battle will take place, but it could be sometime around the middle of the tribulation period. There are some good reasons for believing this, but nothing definitive. Within this passage, only the final three-and-one-half years are mentioned in relation to Israel. Also, as we will see later, it is roughly at the mid-point of the tribulation that literally all hell brakes loose on the earth. Satan becomes much more active in the latter half of the tribulation period through his pawns, the Anti-Christ and the False Prophet. The persecution of Israel and accepters becomes predominant in the world focus.

Satan is going to send some type of an attack against the people of Israel, who will be hiding somewhere in the desert of Jordan. According to Daniel 11:41, the area that is now Jordan will not be taken by Anti-Christ. Revelation 12:16 describes the defeat of this attack as a miraculous event in which God protects Israel. When this attack fails, Satan begins to go after the accepters in the world. Those who have accepted Jesus are the remnants of the woman's seed who have the testimony of Jesus Christ.

This chapter is not the only place Satan is found in Revelation. He is mentioned again in chapter 13, verses 2 and 4. Here he is seen as giving our next character, the Anti-Christ, his power. We have already looked at Revelation 20 where Satan is bound for 1,000 years, released, and then defeated and placed in the lake of fire for eternity.

Satan is a scary, violent figure who hates God with every fiber of his being. He has great power, and is going to unleash it like never before against God's people during the final part of the tribulation period. He will be the one behind the brutality of the one world government led by Anti-Christ. Satan knows he can't win, but with spite, he wants to take as many people with him as he can.

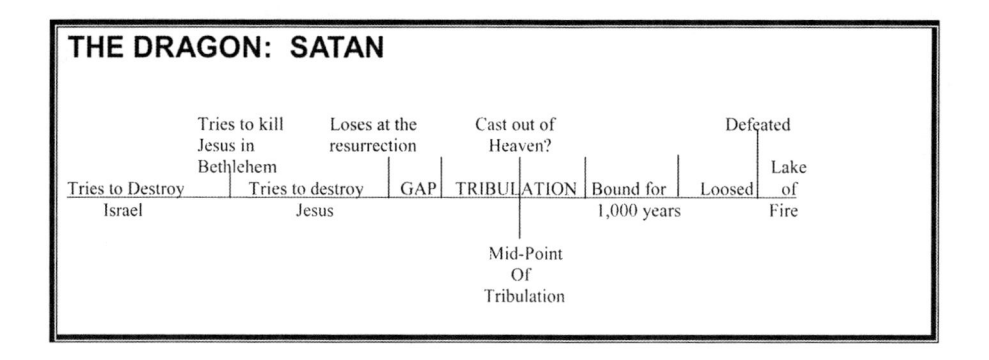

THE DRAGON: SATAN

| Tries to Destroy Israel | Tries to kill Jesus in Bethlehem | Tries to destroy Jesus | Loses at the resurrection | GAP | Cast out of Heaven? TRIBULATION Mid-Point Of Tribulation | Bound for 1,000 years | Loosed | Defeated Lake of Fire |

THE BEAST: ANTI-CHRIST

READ: REVELATION 13:1–10 AND CHAPTER 17 AND DANIEL 7

Now we come to one of the most controversial figures in the Bible. This person is called Anti-Christ, and is only referred to by that name once in 1 John 2:18. He is called this because he is the antitheses of Jesus. Jesus came into the world to save it, this one just wants to rule, and destroy what he cannot have. Jesus was under the power of God the Father, this person will be under the power of Satan.

It is hard to know how to attack this topic. To go straight through the scriptures could be confusing. We have a lot of details about this person and the things he will do, but there is controversy in their interpretation. So, as we go through this section we need to remember that there can be a variance of interpretations on particular points. I am going to try to give you a running outline of the actions of this person, along with the scripture to back it up. But, this is by no means definitive in interpretation.

Revelation 13 tells us that this beast comes up out of the sea. It is generally held in prophetic interpretation that the sea represents humanity. I am sure you have heard the term "sea of humanity." John sees this beast rising from the human population of the earth. This means that he is natural in origin, not supernatural. Jesus was born of a virgin, a supernatural origin. This man will be just a man, born from a mother and a father.

John goes on to describe this beast. As we continue looking at the descriptions of this beast, we must understand something. In the oriental mind, which is what Jews are considered, the king and his kingdom are thought of as one and the same. To talk about a king is to talk about his kingdom, the way he rules and where he rules. So, as John describes this beast, he is not only talking about an individual, but also a government, or kingdom. This is important to understand because the description John gives of the beast in chapters 13 and 17 relate to both the individual and his kingdom.

John describes this beast as having seven heads, ten horns, and ten crowns, with the name of blasphemy on his heads. His body was like a leopard, his feet like a bear, and his mouth like a lion. The dragon is the one who gives him his power to rule. Obviously this beast contains a lot of symbolism, so let us see if we can dissect it.

The body is the easiest place to start. We have to go to the book of Daniel in order to make sense of the body. Daniel records seeing four beasts (Daniel

7). The first beast he saw was like a lion with eagle's wings. It was made to stand like a man. Daniel was heavily influenced by the writings of the prophet Jeremiah. Daniel knew from Jeremiah's writings that the captivity of the Jews in Babylon would end soon. God gave Daniel a vision of a beast that Daniel could identify with. The prophet Jeremiah had described the coming Babylonians as a lion (Jeremiah 4:7), and as an eagle (Jeremiah 4:13). Years before Daniel had told King Nebuchadnezzar, the king of Babylon, that he would go mad and be like an animal until he acknowledged that God was in charge. This happened. Nebuchadnezzar had thought of himself as a god, but after this event, he knew he was just a man. The lion with eagle's wings and a man's heart was representative of the kingdom of Babylon.

The second beast observed by Daniel was like a bear, raised up on one side, with ribs in its mouth. This beast represents the Medo-Persian Empire. The Medes and the Persians formed an alliance, but it was not an equal one. The Persians held the majority of the power, which is why the bear is raised on one side. This Empire was known for its fierceness in battle (the ribs in the teeth). The Medes and the Persians conquered the Babylonians. They were the empire responsible for returning Israel back to its homeland.

The third beast was like a leopard, which had four wings and four heads. This beast represents Greece. Alexander the Great conquered the known world with amazing speed, like a leopard with wings. But, upon his death, his kingdom was divided among four people, the four heads.

The last beast in Daniel's vision was of Rome. It was a terrible beast that crushed everything beneath it. Nothing ruled like Rome, and nothing has since. This beast is shown with ten horns. One of these horns displaces three of the horns, and begins speaking great things. This is a glimpse into Anti-Christ, as the next thing Daniel observes is Jesus coming to set up His kingdom. Daniel sees the beast slain and cast into the lake of fire.

Body of a Leopard—Greece (Dan. 7:6)
Feet of a Bear—Media-Persia (Dan. 7:5)
Mouth of a Lion—Babylon (Dan. 7:4)
Indescribable Beast—Rome

With this background, let us look at Revelation 13:2. The body of this beast has the characteristics of three of the four beasts Daniel saw. Its mouth is like a lion. He will speak like he is god, like Nebuchadnezzar did in Babylon. Its feet are like a bear's. He will have the fierceness in battle like the Medes and

Persians. The body is like a leopard. He will have the speed in conquering the world like Alexander the Great. He has ten horns. Like the Roman Empire, the absolute domination of rule will be his hallmark. This beast, this man and his kingdom, will bear the marks of these great world powers.

The seven heads need to be explained, but for that we must go deeper into the book of Revelation. Chapter 17 gives us a description of a woman sitting on a beast. To keep this simple, let me just say that the woman represents the false religions of the world. The beast is the same beast we have been looking at in chapter 13. We will get back to the woman later when we talk about the kings and the false prophet. For now, let us look at the beast.

In chapter 17, John is given an interpretation of the beast and the woman. This makes it easier for us. Verse 9 tells us that the seven heads are seven mountains on which the woman sits. Many people take this as a reference to Rome, with its seven hills. But the seven heads also seem to represent the seven kings, or kingdoms mentioned in the next verse.

It is said of these kingdoms that five have fallen, one is, and one is yet to come, but only for a short time. The kingdom of the beast is the eighth kingdom. At the time of John's vision, five world powers had controlled Israel, either its land or its people, at some time. One, Rome, was in control at the time of the writing. One more kingdom would have control for a short time before the final kingdom, the beast, would come into power.

I believe we can identify the five kingdoms that had rule over Israel previous to John's writing. If we include just having authority over the people of Israel, then we can start with Egypt as the first country. They held the Jews in bondage for over 400 years. Assyria was the next world power to hold most of the land of Israel by conquering the northern tribes. Babylon finished the job by destroying Judah, the remaining two tribes of Israel, and then taking the land held by the Assyrians. The Medo-Persian Empire conquered Babylon, and took the land. If we are talking about empires only holding the land, these two could be split since the Median Empire started in dominance, then the Persian Empire. If these are split, then Egypt would not count having only held the people of Israel. The fifth empire was Greece.

It is the one that is to come for a short time that is not as easy to determine. The only world empire to control Israel after Rome, and only for a short time, was the British Empire. The British became a world empire in the 1800s, but did not come into possession of the land of Israel until 1918. They held the land for only 30 years before Israel became a state. If the British Empire is the empire yet to come, then the next world empire to have control of Israel will be the Beast. But, nothing says that this interpretation is absolutely right.

There could be another empire between now and the Beast, but it is unlikely. From this interpretation it is believed that the next world empire will be that of the Beast.

> **5 Fallen**—Egypt, Assyria, Babylon, Media-Persia, Greece
> **Or,** Assyria, Babylon, Median Empire, Persian Empire, Greece
> **1 is**—Rome
> **1 is yet to come for a short time**—British Empire
> **The Beast is the Eighth, but of the Seven.** He will rule a world empire.

Those are the basics on the coming world empire of the Beast. It will have characteristics of past empires including ferocity, domination, and swiftness in conquering. It will be global and will have control of the land of Israel. Now let us look at the individual we call the Anti-Christ who will be the leader of this world empire.

First, we have seen ten horns mentioned several times already. These horns, according to Daniel 7:24, are ten leaders. It is believed that there will be a ten-member confederation that is formed containing some of the area of the old Roman Empire. People have gone crazy trying to figure out a modern correlation to these ten leaders and their countries. Many theories have already fallen by the way side, but some are still probable. It does not serve the purpose of this book to go through these theories. The fact is that there will be a ten-member confederation. From this group a lower level leader will rise in power and will displace three of the leaders when he comes to power. This group of ten leaders will then become the support group for this new leader, backing his leadership, and controlling the world.

The fall of the three leaders may be violent, or may be accomplished by stealth, but it will give this Anti-Christ the power he needs. He will be in a position, according to Daniel 9:27, to make a treaty with Israel for seven years. This treaty will be for protection from Israel's enemies, which means he has the military might to protect them. It is the signing of this treaty which begins the seventieth week of Daniel, the seven years of tribulation.

Halfway through this seven year period things get very interesting in relation to this world leader. Several things happen in rapid succession. It is not made clear in scripture as to the sequence of events, but we can get an idea by knowing how things usually work in this world. The first thing that will take place is a resurrection of a dead Anti-Christ. Revelation 13:3 and 14 tells us that this man will suffer a fatal head wound, but he will live. Everyone in the world will see this as a miracle, and some will begin to worship him. But Satan is the one who actually heals him. It is from Satan's power that this man rules and lives.

Next in succession is probably the defeat of Anti-Christ's archenemies, the two witnesses, whom we will study later. This world ruler is the only person who can kill these two men (Revelation 11:7).

This thrilling victory gives Anti-Christ a surge of adrenaline and leads to the second act. He enters the rebuilt temple in Jerusalem and declares himself to be the one and only God. This event is spoken of in more prophetic writings in the Bible than any other event related to this man (Daniel 9:27;11:31–35; 12:11; Matthew 24:15; 2 Thessalonians 2:4; Revelation 13:4–6). It is called the abomination of desecration, or desolation. It is the one event that will identify this man as truly being Anti-Christ. Remember that I speculated that Satan was cast out of heaven at about this time in the tribulation period. It is believed that Satan actually takes possession of this man as he sets himself up as god in the temple. From this point on, the gloves are off.

The next step for this ruler is to break his treaty with Israel. Obviously those of the Jewish faith would take exception to this man making himself god. There may be some sort of revolt against him, which he can claim as an excuse to break the treaty. But, with Satan empowering him, he does not need any motivation to go against Israel. The Jews go into hiding as persecution begins.

We will get into the religious side of the Anti-Christ when we discuss his chief henchman, the False Prophet. For now, let us run toward the end of the story. The Beast (Anti-Christ), empowered by the Dragon (Satan), and helped by the False Prophet, gathers the armies of the world together at the valley of Megiddo in the northern part of Israel (Revelation 16:13–16). He convinces the people that they can fight God and win. This battle is known as Armageddon. It is not man versus man with atomic weapons; it is man versus God. As we will see in the next chapter, it doesn't last long, and it is doubtful man ever gets a shot off. The finale of the battle is the capture of the Beast. He is thrown alive into the lake of fire (Daniel 11:45; 7:11, 26; Revelation 19:20). This man who proclaimed himself to be god did not last long against the real God.

Let me just sum up what we have found out about this man we call Anti-Christ. He will come into power by overthrowing three leaders in a ten-member confederacy. He will set up a world empire that will have the characteristics of four other world empires. He will be the sole leader of the world, and will be empowered by Satan. The protection treaty he signs with Israel will start the clock on the seven years of tribulation, but he breaks this treaty after only three-and-a-half years. He is able to defeat God's messengers, the two witnesses, and then sets himself up to be god. In a desperate attempt to defeat God he gathers all the armies of the world to Megiddo. He loses badly and is cast into the lake of fire for eternity. Daniel 7:11–14 also tells us that the millennial reign of Jesus on the earth will be after the Beast is defeated.

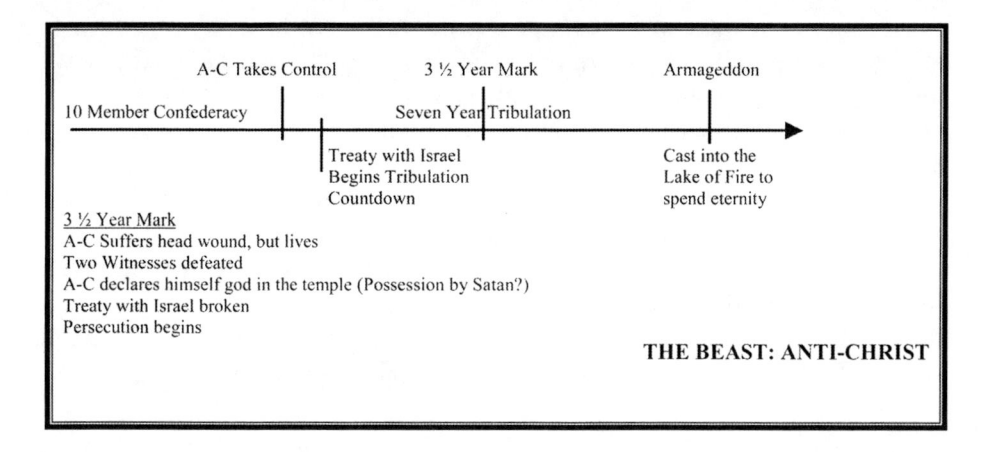

```
                    A-C Takes Control        3 ½ Year Mark              Armageddon
10 Member Confederacy      |                       |                         |
                           |———————Seven Year Tribulation———————————————————|————►
                           |Treaty with Israel                       Cast into the
                           |Begins Tribulation                       Lake of Fire to
                           |Countdown                                spend eternity
3 ½ Year Mark
A-C Suffers head wound, but lives
Two Witnesses defeated
A-C declares himself god in the temple (Possession by Satan?)
Treaty with Israel broken
Persecution begins
                                                          THE BEAST: ANTI-CHRIST
```

THE BEAST FROM THE EARTH: THE FALSE PROPHET

READ: REVELATION 13:11–18; 19:20

The final character in our gruesome threesome is the False Prophet. This man will rise to prominence promoting the religion of the Beast. As the tribulation begins there is a religion which will be prevalent in the world, and which will ride on the back of the Anti-Christ (the woman from Revelation 17). This religion will be promoted and upheld by the Beast and the ten leaders, until it no longer serves their purpose.

Probably around the time that the Beast declares himself to be god, the ten world leaders will go against this false religion and begin promoting the religion of the Beast. They will destroy the false religion. At this point there will be a single spokesman for the Beast, his prophet. This man will be able to perform miracles in order to get people to worship the Beast. He will set up images of the Anti-Christ and force people to worship them. He will even be able to make one image appear to be alive.

The religion of the Beast will be the one world religion. When you think about it, it fits right in with the prevailing philosophy of the modern age. Man is god. How perfect it is to have a religion where a man has become god? It lines up with many of the eastern religions, and cults, and even the new age mysticism. This is the fully evolved man. This is the god man was meant to be. Unfortunately it will be easy pickings for the False Prophet.

When you say the number 666, people think about it being a Satanic symbol. Well, this number comes from Revelation 13:18. It is considered the number of the Beast, yet no one really understands what it is, or what it means. I suppose when it comes into play during the tribulation people will understand. But, the significance of this number is found in the surrounding passage.

The False Prophet sets up the world so that no one can buy or sell anything in the world without a mark in their right hand or their forehead. This mark is to signify that you worship the Beast. Those who do not worship the Beast will not be able to conduct trade, and they will be killed. The mark will consist of either the name of the Beast, or his number, which is 666. This is a horrible thing to think about, and why some people are almost superstitious about this number.

We do not know what form this mark will take, and there is a lot of speculation even today. What is certain is that the people will fully understand what this mark is for. It is a mark of loyalty to the Beast. There will be no gray area as people fully understand that they are devoting themselves to the Beast when they take this mark. Accepting the mark seals your place in the lake of fire as you once and for all decide against God. By this point in the tribulation people will have heard both sides and know they have to choose between God or the Beast.

The False Prophet ends up swimming with the Beast in the lake of fire forever (Revelation 19:20). He deceives many people on earth into following this man, and ends up deceiving even himself.

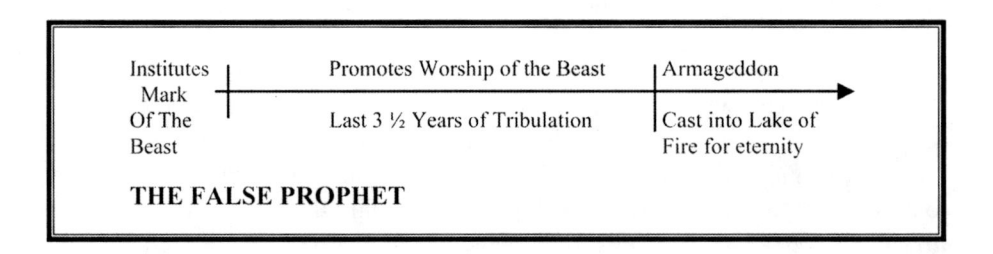

Institutes Mark Of The Beast	Promotes Worship of the Beast Last 3 ½ Years of Tribulation	Armageddon Cast into Lake of Fire for eternity

THE FALSE PROPHET

The three characters we have just studied form what some call the unholy trinity. The holy trinity is God the Father, God the Son, and God the Holy Spirit. This unholy trinity is Satan, the Beast, and the False Prophet. Each is a counter to their holy opposites. Satan desires to be the Father, and mimics His actions in supplying power to the Beast. The Beast, as we have seen, is the antitheses of Jesus the Son. The False Prophet points people to the Beast, just like the Holy Spirit points people to the Son. Satan cannot create on his own, he always seems to have to imitate, or twist, what God does.

THE TRINITIES

UNHOLY TRINITY	HOLY TRINITY
THE DRAGON: *SATAN*	**GOD THE FATHER**
THE BEAST: *ANTI-CHRIST*	**GOD THE SON, JESUS**
THE FALSE PROPHET	**THE HOLY SPIRIT**

The holiness of God will be fighting against the evil of these three and their followers during the tribulation period. The refusers during this time, who follow the Beast, will hate God, and will shake their fists at Him and curse Him for the plagues that He is sending to earth. They will continue to follow the Beast and Satan, even though God demonstrates that He is more powerful. They will continue to blame God for their punishment even though God gives them messengers to let them know the truth about His grace. All refusers have to do is turn to God, but they will not.

THE GOOD GUYS

THE TWO WITNESSES

READ: REVELATION 11:3–13

Now we come to my favorite characters in this tribulation drama. The two witnesses are the spokespeople for God during the first part of the tribulation. They are associated with the temple in Jerusalem, but are not necessarily chained to it. They can move around, but the temple will probably be their home base. These men will be like the Old Testament prophets, pointing people to Jesus. They will proclaim their message for 1,260 days (three and a half years). Their clothes will be made of sackcloth, a very course material resembling burlap.

These two are referred to as the two olive trees and candlesticks standing before God. This leads us to Zechariah 4. Here the prophet Zechariah sees a vision of a candlestick, which is a pole with seven bowls on it to hold oil. Two olive trees are beside this lamp stand, feeding oil into it. This is a vision about sharing the light of God with others. The original receivers of this message were rebuilding the temple after the Persians allowed them back into their homeland. God was telling them that they were displaying His power by building the temple, and that the temple would be used to tell others about Him. These two witnesses in Revelation are going to be light bearers for God. Their power will come from the Holy Spirit like the lamp's power came from the olive tree.

These men are not going to be preaching a popular message. They are going to be telling people that Jesus is the real Messiah, something the Jewish religion does not accept. They will uphold Jesus as God, something other religions do not accept. God is not going to be popular during this time. God is going to perform miracles through these men and because of these men.

In order to protect them, God is going to burn up anyone who tries to hurt them. This fire will come out of their mouths. It makes us think about Elijah in 2 Kings 1:10–15. He had just sent word to the king of Israel that God said the king was going to die from injuries he had received. The king was not happy about this and sent soldiers to bring Elijah to him. They were apparently going to take him by force. Fifty men came to Elijah, and the captain told him to come with him. Elijah spoke and fire came down and burned up the captain and his fifty men. A second team of fifty suffered the same fate as the first. The third captain however, was smart. He humbled himself and asked Elijah to spare his life, and then asked politely that Elijah come with him to the king. Elijah went. Whoever tries to hurt these two witnesses will suffer the same death by fire as the first two groups of people who tried to force Elijah to go to the king.

These men can also keep it from raining, which is also something Elijah did (1 Kings 17:1; 18:41–45). It did not rain in Israel for three and a half years, until Elijah prayed that it would rain. Interestingly enough, this is the same amount of time that the Witnesses are supposed to be proclaiming their message and performing miracles.

Turning water into blood was one of the plagues God sent against the Egyptians through Moses when Pharoah did not want to let them go free (Exodus 7:20). These men will also be able to do that. Imagine having no rain, so water is scarce already, and then, the water you do have turns to blood. The Witnesses will also be able to cause other plagues like Moses (Exodus 8:1–12:29).

Some people think that these men will be Moses and Elijah returned to earth. Outside of the similarity in miracles, there is no evidence that this is true. The miracles are similar because it is the same God performing them. God wants the people to know it is Him, the same God Who performed miracles through the great prophets Moses and Elijah. There is no benefit to bringing these men back, no one would know what they look like anyway. I believe these are two new prophets, specifically sent for this time in history.

These men are not going to perform these miracles and unleash these plagues just for the fun of it. They are designed to show the power and authority of God. It is hoped that people will believe their message when they see these miracles, just like they believe the False Prophet when he does his miracles. But, when people do not want to accept God, then they will be given a small taste of God's holiness against them. This is going to make these men the most hated, and most wanted in the world.

Only one person will be able to kill the Witnesses, and then only at the right time. After their 1260 days are over, then Anti-Christ, the Beast, will kill these men. They have caused such widespread hardship all over the world with their plagues that the entire world will have a party to celebrate their deaths. Think of the celebrations that take place in countries where cruel dictators have been overthrown, or killed. People are usually dancing in the streets. These men will be hated by the entire world far more than any dictator has ever been hated. Their bodies will remain in the street where they were killed, untouched and unburied. News broadcasts all over the world will carry pictures of their dead bodies so people can be certain that they are dead and it is not some hoax by the world government.

But, the party will be cut short. Halfway through the fourth day, the Witnesses stand up and brush themselves off. Can you see the look on the reporter's face who is broadcasting live from the dead bodies in Jerusalem? As the crowd of onlookers, who have come to gawk at the bodies themselves, sees them rise, fear and panic begin to spread. All over the world people are seeing these hated men rise up from the dead as television cameras catch every moment. Then, a voice from the sky tells the men to come up, and they begin to rise into the clouds like Jesus.

After this a great earthquake hits Jerusalem and causes one-third of the city to fall and seven thousand people are killed. Those Jews who survive the quake believe the two Witnesses were from God, and they give praise to God because of it. So, the final miracle convinced them.

THE 144,000

READ: REVELATION 7:1–8; 14:1–5

Much is made of the 144,000. In fact, at least one group has made it the center of their doctrine. So, who are these 144,000 people, and what is their purpose, or function, within the stream of tribulation events? There really is not much written about them, but I believe we can get a clear picture from the scriptures we just read.

Chapter seven shows us that these people are to be sealed with the seal of God. This is counter to the mark of the beast. The belief that this sealing takes place at the front end of the tribulation period is almost unanimous. The angels with the plagues are being restrained from launching their attack against the earth until these people are properly identified and marked.

These people are called "the servants of our God" (7:3). They "follow the Lamb (Jesus) wherever He goes" (14:4). These people are accepters. They have accepted Jesus as the payment for their sin, and live their life according to His words and leadership. This is what it means when it says that they are without fault (14:5). They share their faith with others, and spread the truth of God wherever He leads them.

Chapter seven tells us that these people are all Jewish. Twelve thousand people from each of the twelve tribes are sealed. This means that not a single person is sealed with this protective seal of God who is not Jewish. This also means that there will be 144,000 Jews who accept Jesus as their Messiah, and accept His payment for their sin. It could be that the teaching of the two Witnesses sparks an awakening among the Jews, particularly with this group. It is doubtful that any Jewish person today can be sure of what tribe he fits into since so much scattering has happened in their history. But God knows who belongs to what tribe, and He will see to it that 12,000 come from each of the tribes.

We find out more details about these people in chapter 14. Some of the details are hard for us to believe, but they will undoubtedly be true. Verse 4 starts out with the fact that these people have not been defiled with women, then clarifies this point by saying they are virgins. This means that the 144,000 are all men. And, yes, virgin means never had sex with a woman. The Greek word is *parthenos* and it is the same word used for Mary when she was told she was going to have a child. This word means exactly what our word virgin means.

There are some who say that finding 144,000 males who are virgins, even Jewish, would be impossible in today's world, so this could not possibly mean what it says. But, it is not as impossible as we might think. I can think of a couple of scenarios where this could be true. First, they are all young men who are just reaching puberty, around the age of thirteen or fourteen, when they are sealed. Even if they lived until the end of the tribulation they would only be 21. Their commitment to Jesus would keep them from taking time for personal relationships with the opposite sex.

Another way this could be possible is if there was a religious order of the Jews set up similar to our monastery system. These young men could be cloistered away in different places, or the order could be celibate and they still live in their own homes. This is not as far fetched as it may seem. There is precedence for strict sects to arise from within Judaism. Such a sect could take on the rights of the Nazarite found in the Old Testament, which would be strict, even to the diet. This sect could also be searching for the truth about Messiah, and would then easily have their eyes opened to the truth by the Witnesses. Of course, this is all conjecture. No one really knows how this is all going to come about, but we can be sure that these men will be virgins like God says.

The word "firstfruits" is used to describe these men in verse 4. This word has a long history in the Bible. Firstfruits was used to mean the first of the fruit, or animals, that would be given to God as a sacrifice. It was also used to denote the best of the fruit or harvest. Either meaning could be true of these gentlemen. They were the best in their commitment to Jesus and their lifestyle, according to their description. And, as we will see, they were the first in an awakening of people in Israel and around the world to Jesus.

The New Testament uses the word "firstfruits" on several occasions to show relationship in time. Jesus is the first of those who will be resurrected (1 Corinthians 15:20–23). It is used of a person to declare them as the first accepters in a region (Romans 16:5; 1 Corinthians 16:15). If this passage in Revelation is referring to the 144,000 as the first people to accept Jesus, then it brings up some interesting questions.

There must have been some change to happen, something new must be occurring, or these men could not be the first to experience it, or to do it. The change would have to do with accepting Jesus because they are listed as "firstfruits unto God and to the Lamb." But, there have been accepters since the resurrection of Jesus. Why would these men be any different? How could they be the first of the accepters?

On the other hand, if the word "firstfruits" is speaking of quality, it still brings up questions. Out of the millions of people who have accepted Jesus as the payment for their sin, who are not of Jewish descent and have lived a life that is honoring to God, how is it that 144,000 Jewish men are singled out as being the best of the best? What makes them more special than a non-Jew who suffered persecution in a Muslim, or Communist, country because of their faith?

The huge, glaring question that comes out in studying the 144,000 is; where is the church? Where are the millions of accepters that now live all over the world? Why is it that only these 144,000 Jewish men are singled out as being the only servants of God on earth (7:3)? Why are they called the "firstfruits" when there are already so many others on this earth who are living their lives for Jesus? What has happened to the church we now know on this earth? The answers will come later in our study.

This sealing of the 144,000 comes at the beginning of the tribulation period, and seals these people with the mark of God on their foreheads for special protection from the plagues to come. The 144,000 are Jewish males, with 12,000 from each of the twelve tribes, who are virgins and have accepted Jesus as the payment for their sin. They live an exemplary life, representing God well as they proclaim His message of grace to those on the earth during the tribulation period.

THE GREAT MULTITUDE

READ: REVELATION 7:9–17

In this passage we see the greatest expression of God's grace. John sees a great multitude from every country and ethnic background in the world. We are told that these people are accepters who came out of the great tribulation. The term "great tribulation" can only mean the seven-year period of God venting His holy anger on the world. This term is usually reserved for the final half of the seven-year period when Anti-Christ is hunting down the people of God to kill them. At no other time in the history of the world will it be harder to be an accepter, anywhere in the world.

These people will live through the darkest time in human history. Everything on earth will be against them, to keep them from wanting to accept Jesus. But God demonstrates His grace by bringing them through it. He opens up the gate of truth by sending out the 144,000 with His message. After seven years, there is a large multitude of people who accept Jesus and reject the false religion of the beast.

These people accept Jesus during the tribulation, but not all of them make it through this period alive. Many will die, martyred for their faith in Jesus. Some will live until the time Jesus returns, and enter into the millennial kingdom.

When they enter the eternal state, they will serve God continuously in His temple. All the pain and suffering they went through during the persecution on earth will be gone forever. They could not buy food because they did not have the mark of the beast, but God will feed them now. Water was scarce, but they will have plenty now. They could not live in homes, so they lived exposed to the elements. God will shelter them now. All the tears they cried for their own pain and the pain of others will be wiped away. They will have no reason to cry for sorrow, only for joy.

If the 144,000 are the firstfruits of a group, then this is the group. It is through the spread of the gospel by these Jewish evangelists that this great multitude hears the good news and responds. This group accepts Jesus during the hardest time in human history, and yet they come out victorious through the grace of God.

READ: REVELATION 14:6–13

This passage is a good summary of what we have studied in this chapter, and a great demonstration of the difference between God's grace and holiness. The first part, verses six through eight, is God showing His grace to the people on the earth. He offers them a chance to accept Him. He gives them the two Witnesses and the 144,000 to spread His good news all over the earth. A great multitude of people accept Jesus. While these people may have to endure the anger of Satan and his Anti-Christ, they will not have to suffer the wrath of God.

Then there are verses nine through twelve. This talks about the holiness of God being poured out in anger on those who follow the Beast. Those who refuse God and think that Satan, the Beast, and the False Prophet offer the best way to live. All of them will end up destroyed. They will be thrown into a lake of fire where they will burn forever and ever. Anyone who takes the mark of the beast will doom themselves to an eternity of torture. They will have refused God's presence in their life forever.

God showers the great multitude of people who accept Him with His grace, especially the two Witnesses and the 144,000. But God also pours out His wrath on the unholy trinity of Satan, the Beast, and the False Prophet, along with those who follow them. God's grace and holiness are eternal.

MIND THE GAP

The unholy trinity is just the consummation of players that try to influence us everyday to step away from God. There is not a day that goes by that a friend, a parent, an organization, or the world at large does not try to get us to believe that there is no God, or if there is, that we do not have to follow Him. This is exactly what Satan wants.

There are only two camps we can belong to in this epic struggle. If we are not a part of Gods camp, then we are by default a part of Satan's. All Satan has to do is keep us from entering a relationship with God. In order to accomplish that, all he has to do is lie.

During the tribulation, Satan will spread the lie that Anti-Christ is god. In our present age, he spreads the lie that there is no God. There is no Creator, we simply came into being. He tells us that we are able to make our own decisions, come to our own conclusions, about morality. We do not need to consult with God about what is right and wrong. He whispers to us that, while the entire world is a cesspool, we are good people and do not need the guilt trip that we have sinned and caused someone's death to pay for it. He makes us laugh about hell and caricatures of him. It is easy to not believe in something when you laugh at it. Then it becomes nothing more than a fairy tale. If there is no devil, then there is no antithesis called God.

At the same time all of this is going on, there are a few accepters out there trying to spread the truth to counteract the lies. Just like in the tribulation period where we see the two witnesses and the 144,000, there are people in communities around the globe who try to share the truth of God with others. Accepters fight an uphill battle against the lies of Satan. There are many lies, only one truth.

In the end, the war will be won by the accepters. But each day brings its own battles. Person by person a little ground is conquered. A relationship is built. And Satan loses one more from his camp.

The Tribulation Plot

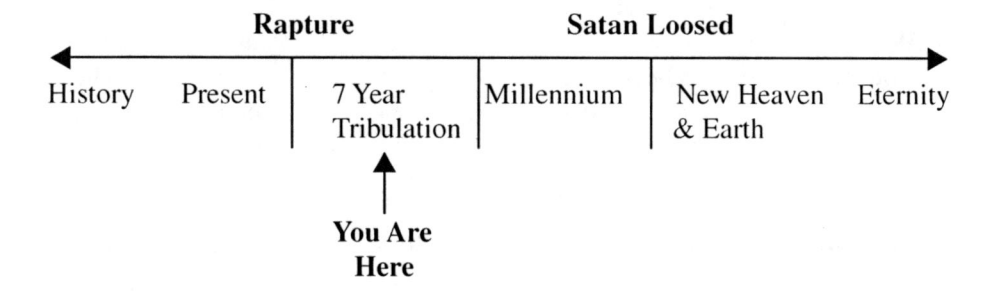

```
              Rapture        Satan Loosed
◄─────────────┬─────────┬──────────────┬──────────►
History  Present  7 Year    Millennium  New Heaven  Eternity
                  Tribulation            & Earth
                      ↑
                  You Are
                   Here
```

In the last chapter we looked at the players in this tribulation drama. Now we are going to delve into the plot. We are going to see the action that takes place, the devastating events that culminate in the return of Jesus to set up His millennial kingdom. The description of these events is found in the book of Revelation, with some supporting verses found elsewhere in the Bible. Not even the most noted horror writer could come up with a plot like this one.

THE SEAL JUDGMENTS

> **READ: REVELATION 6:1–17; 8:1 AND MATTHEW 24:1–31**

Previously we discussed the Apostle John being taken to the throne room of God. While there he caught a glimpse of God's holiness and grace. He saw the holiness of God on His throne, but he saw the grace of God in Jesus, represented by a lamb that had been slaughtered.

Within the throne room passage of Revelation 5, an interesting item is introduced. A scroll has been written on both sides, and has seven seals. These seals would have been on the outside edge of the roll, and would only allow so much of the scroll to be unrolled at one time. No one in heaven or earth was found worthy to open the scroll. But then Jesus came on the scene. He was worthy.

This scroll is the plot, or plan, for the purification of the earth. It is the lay out of the judgment against man and his sin. It shows the preparations that must be made in order for Jesus to take His rightful place as King on this earth. Only Jesus can open this scroll, because only Jesus lived a perfect life and died to pay the price for sin. Jesus is the only One Who has the right to give out judgment against sin. This right was given to Him by God the Father. As each one of the seals is opened, another judgment, or part of the plan, is realized on earth.

THE FIRST SEAL

As Jesus opens the first seal, John observes a rider coming on a white horse. This rider had a bow, and a crown was given to him, and he went out conquering. He is the lead off man for the four horsemen of the Apocolypse, a term you may have run across in some other place. If you are scratching your head right now wondering what that is about, don't worry. Many great Bible scholars have struggled with the passages we are about to look at. Hopefully we can make some sense out of it. I believe the key is to try to not get too detailed.

A white horse was a symbol of power and authority. Conquering Roman generals would parade through the streets riding a white horse and having the spoils of war follow behind them. But this rider did not earn his position by himself, it was given to him. He was given a crown, a position of leadership. That begs the question of who gave him this authority? But, we will discuss this later. He went out and conquered. We can assume he conquered people and land. How did he conquer? He conquered with a bow. Notice there are no arrows, or quiver, mentioned. This rider conquers peacefully. He threatens, but it is a peaceful take over.

THE SECOND SEAL

When the second seal is opened John sees a rider coming on a red horse. This rider is given the ability to take peace from the earth, and he is given a huge sword. Again, this begs the question, who gave him the sword and the authority? When this rider comes into play there will be wars on the earth. The peaceful takeovers initiated by the rider of the white horse will escalate into conflict and war.

THE THIRD SEAL

With war follows famine, and with the opening of the third seal John sees the rider of the black horse. This rider has a pair of balancing scales in his hand, like a merchant would use to measure out his product of wheat or barley. Ordinarily a penny would have been a day's wage for a rural worker, and would have bought about eight times as much wheat and barley as is listed in the scripture. This scripture tells us that there will be an extreme shortage of food as people will work all day just to buy enough food for one day.

The oil and wine were not to be hurt. Oil would be necessary for making the bread with the grain, and the wine would be necessary for drinking when water was not available. Shortages of food, and a tainted water supply are major problems following a war.

THE FOURTH SEAL

Of all the horsemen, this is the most feared. His name is Death, and he is riding a pale horse. Pale could mean that the horse was a greenish color, or that it looked sickly, like death was about to overtake it. Following Death was Hades, the temporary holding place of the refusers who die. One quarter of the population of the earth is going to die with the plagues these two manifest. They will kill through violence (sword), with famine (hunger), with disease (death), and even with animals. This is the anchor leg of the four horsemen, and by far the worst.

Let us pause here and discuss these four horsemen. Who are they? What is their purpose? This topic has been the subject of much debate, so allow me to just give you my opinion on the matter.

Many people hold that the first horseman, the rider on the white horse, is Anti-Christ, the Beast. This may explain the first rider, but it does not explain the rest. All of the riders seem to be cut from the same cloth, they are all similar. These could be merely representations of events which will happen, but then, why would it be necessary to assign riders, personal beings, to each event?

As was stated in the first chapter, I believe that the scriptures interpret themselves better than we can. So, do these four horsemen show up anywhere else in scripture? I believe they do. In the Old Testament book of Zechariah (one book removed from the end of the Old Testament), the prophet sees a vision of horsemen, not once, but twice.

Riders are first seen in Zechariah 1:8–11. Here the prophet sees a rider on a red horse. He asks the messenger angel with him who this is. The angel replies that this is an angelic being sent by the Lord to keep watch over the earth. The rider reports that the earth is at peace. This rider's responsibility was simply to observe what was happening in this world, not to interfere. His orders came from God.

The riders are seen again, but this time with chariots connected to the horses (Zechariah 6:1–8). Here we see horses that are red, black, white, and some with spots of color. These riders are also sent out by God into the earth to perform some task. We are not told specifically what task they perform, although verse eight insinuates that those going to the north have performed some act of justice against the country of the north, Babylon.

I believe that the riders Zechariah saw are the same riders that John saw. They are angelic beings who are sent by God to perform certain duties in relation to earth. This time the mission of each rider is clear. God gives the first rider his crown, and the second rider his sword. These would be necessary to carry out their mission. The fourth rider's name could literally be Death, as in the angel of death.

So, what exactly is their mission? Before I answer that question let me say that I do not think that those who believe the first rider to be Anti-Christ are far off. It seems to me that all of the seal judgments relate in some way to Anti-Christ and his kingdom. This would be supported by the passages we read in

Zechariah where the context is these angelic beings watching over the earthly kingdom of Babylon, and even taking part in its destruction. That is why I believe that the mission of these riders is to help Anti-Christ come to power. Then they are to bring about the consequences of the people placing Anti-Christ in power. In other words, God is going to use these riders to give people what they want, a king of the world who has nothing to do with God. Then He will use the riders to give people the consequences of their choice.

The four seals should play out something like this. God will allow Anti-Christ to begin building his power base of countries peacefully (white horse). He gains the leadership of the ten-member confederacy. Other countries will join him. Eventually God will cause some countries, or areas, to resist, and they will be dealt with through force (red horse). God will see to it that this war causes a world-wide famine (black horse). As the rider of the pale horse arrives, God will see to it that all of the plagues and devastation associated with war and conflict will come on the Anti-Christ's kingdom. One quarter of the population of the world, which Anti-Christ rules, will be killed by diseases, violence, starvation, and even wild animals.

We must always keep in mind that God is the one Who is in control. He is the One Who sets up kings and kingdoms. Anti-Christ would not be able to come to power without God allowing it. God will give the people what they want during the tribulation period, but He will also give them the full consequences of that choice.

THE FIFTH SEAL

The fifth seal introduces a change. John sees souls under the altar in heaven. These are the souls of accepters who have been killed because they believed in Jesus. The altar was a place of sacrifice to God. These martyrs gave of themselves as a sacrifice to God.

During the last half of the tribulation period, many people will be killed by the government of Anti-Christ because they do not follow him. Remember the mark of the beast instituted by the False Prophet? Those killed during this time will have their body go to the grave on earth, but their soul/spirit will go to heaven.

John sees these people as crying out to God for revenge. They want the people on earth to pay for killing them. They want God to exert His holiness with massive anger, and destroy those on earth. But God tells them to wait. More will be coming who will die because of their acceptance of Jesus. God knows when the time will be right to truly judge the people of the earth, and especially Anti-Christ and his False Prophet. God is also showing mercy on those who may not have committed to Him yet. He wants to give them a little more time to accept Jesus.

THE SIXTH SEAL

Total devastation is the best way to describe this seal. The events listed here are also found in the Old Testament books of Isaiah and Joel. God has finally had enough. He begins with a great earthquake that shakes the whole earth. All the mountains and islands are moved. Islands disappear and mountains are leveled. This is just on the earth.

In space, the sun is darkened. John describes it as being as black as cloth made from black goat's hair. With the sun no longer providing the light for it to reflect, the moon becomes blood red. There is a large meteor shower that strikes the whole earth, and the stars are destroyed. John describes the destruction of the stars like someone rolling up a scroll. It begins from one end and darkens all the way to the other. All the stars are snuffed out. There is nothing left in space beyond the earth, and its moon. Everything is dark.

The people on the earth, regardless of social status, are running and screaming and trying to hide. They would prefer to be crushed by the rocks of the falling mountains than to have to face God and Jesus. This is interesting. These people know about God and Jesus, yet they will not submit themselves to Them. They would rather die than place their lives under the control of God. How sad that the people God loved enough to come to earth and die for, will not allow Him to love them.

THE SEVENTH SEAL

This seal is a bit of a mystery. After a brief parenthesis in which he told about the 144,000 and the great multitude, John finally tells about the final seal. When it is opened there is silence in heaven for about half an hour.

No one really understands what this means. Why is there silence in heaven? It is a complete reversal of the scene we saw in Revelation chapters 4 and 5, where there is loud praise for God. Why silence? We just don't know. God does not see fit to allow John to elaborate on the matter as he moves right on to the next set of judgments.

THE SEALS COMPARED TO MATTHEW 24

During the final week of Jesus, He was in Jerusalem with His disciples. As they exited the temple for what would be His final time, the disciples began showing Jesus the beauty of the buildings. Jesus stopped them in their tracks by declaring that all of those buildings would be destroyed. This upset the disciples because Jerusalem was their capital, and for it to be destroyed meant there would be trouble for Israel ahead. So, they asked Jesus a threefold question. First, they wanted to know when Jerusalem was going to be destroyed. It appears Jesus does not answer this question.

The disciples wanted to know what would be the sign of Jesus' coming. At this point the disciples did not understand about the death and resurrection of Jesus. They believed He was the coming King and would be setting up His kingdom shortly. But, this destruction of Jerusalem thing had them baffled. Would Jerusalem be destroyed before Jesus became king, or after? The third question is tied to the second, even though the disciples did not realize it. When is the end of the world?

Jesus answers the last two questions fairly specifically. No one knows when exactly all this will happen, no dates are set, but the sequence of events has been set. Jesus relates the entire sequence of events for the tribulation period, culminating in His return as King to rule the earth for at least 1,000 years. So, let us look at how Jesus described the tribulation period compared to the description we see in the seal judgments.

As an introduction to the sequence Jesus begins by talking about false Christs who will rise up and deceive people. We see this even today with cult leaders. Some people even follow these false Christs to their death. This will increase the closer we get to the end, with the ultimate false Christ being Anti-Christ.

Verse six begins the actual sequence. We need to remember that Jesus is directing His comments toward the people of Israel. The events He describes will be in relation to those people who live in Israel at the time of the tribulation. These people will hear of wars and rumors of wars. These are not real wars, just talk of them, and threats of war. (The rider of the white horse had no arrows, just a bow.) This statement by Jesus could be referring to the peaceful takeover by Anti-Christ in establishing his power base. This should really not be a concern to anyone in Israel at that time.

After the peaceful takeover is finished, then nations will rise against nations, and kingdoms against kingdoms. There will be a war against the Anti-Christ. Either there will be a revolt by member nations, or a resistance by nations he is trying to conquer. Either way, the rider of the red horse takes peace from the world and launches it into a devastating war.

The consequences of the war are famines and diseases, and Jesus adds earthquakes as well. That sounds like the combined efforts of the riders of the black and pale horses. Jesus says that these are just the beginning. Israel is going to suffer a lot more.

Jesus then begins to talk about the persecution the people of Israel are going to suffer. This would also include the accepters during the tribulation, and would correlate with the souls under the altar in the fifth seal. Jesus gives this description in verses 9–28. The key signal is the abomination of desolation by Anti-Christ in the temple. When the people of Israel see this, they are to run and hide as fast as they can.

The phrase Jesus uses shows exactly how dire this persecution is going to be, and how swift it will come. Jesus tells the people not to come down from their roof and gather up anything, but to just flee. In many areas of Israel houses are built so that you can run from one roof to another, and not have to come down until you reach the edge of town. It is a great method of escape. The beginning of the persecution will be so swift that no one will have time to prepare for it. It will be so harsh that not even expectant mothers will be spared.

This persecution is what begins the great tribulation. It is at this point that God is pouring out all his anger on those who follow Anti-Christ; and Anti-Christ is pouring out his anger on those who follow God. No one is happy, no one is safe. The world has never seen such a time of trouble, anger, and discord. That is why it is called the great tribulation.

Verse 29 gives us a frame of reference as to the sequence of events. It says that after the tribulation, or right at the end, is when the sun will be darkened, the moon will stop shining, the stars will fall, and everything will be shaken. This sounds like the description of the sixth seal. This would mean that the sixth seal falls at the end of the tribulation period.

At this point some sign appears in the heavens, and everyone on earth knows that Jesus is coming. Maybe the silence of the seventh seal is a time of preparation for this event. As the armies of heaven prepare to return with Jesus to conquer the earth, and take it away from the Anti-Christ and Satan. Perhaps the seventh seal is the quiet following the thunder, and the calm before the next rumble pierces the sky.

It appears that the description of the seal judgments falls right in line with the description Jesus gave of the tribulation period in Matthew. From beginning to the second coming, Jesus lays it out for us step by step, and the seals follow right along.

SEAL JUDGMENTS

SEAL	DESCRIPTION	OTHER SCRIPTURE
ONE REVELATION 6:1–2	White horse: Rider with a bow and a crown, conquering peacefully.	MATTHEW 24:6 ZECHARIAH 1:8–11 ZECHARIAH 6:3–6, 8
TWO REVELATION 6:3–4	Red horse: Rider is given the power to take away peace, and a great sword.	MATTHEW 24:7A ZECHARIAH 1:8–11 ZECHARIAH 6:2–5
THREE REVELATION 6:5–6	Black horse: Rider has a pair of balances; high prices for basic food.	MATTHEW 24:7B ZECHARIAH 6:2–8
FOUR REVELATION 6:7–8	Pale horse: Rider is Death, Hell follows him. They are given power over ¼ of the earth to kill with sword, hunger, death, and beasts.	MATTHEW 24:7B ZECHARIAH 1:8–11 ZECHARIAH 6:3–7 1 CHRONICLES 21:14–27
FIVE REVELATION 6:9–11	Souls under the altar.	MATTHEW 24:9–28
SIX REVELATION 6:12–17	Great earthquake, sun darkened, moon as blood, stars fall, heavens depart, every island moved. People hide.	MATTHEW 24:29–31 ISAIAH 2:19–21 ISAIAH 13:10 ISAIAH 24:19–23 ISAIAH 34:4 JOEL 2:31; 3:15
SEVEN REVELATION 8:1	Silence in heaven for about half an hour.	NO OTHER SCRIPTURES SPEAK OF THIS.

THE TRUMPET JUDGMENTS

READ: REVELATION 8:7–9:21; 11:15–19

As the seal judgments end, John sees seven angels with trumpets about to sound. As each angel plays a blast on his trumpet, a judgment takes place on the earth. The focus of the seal judgments appeared to be the government of Anti-Christ and the consequences of that government. The trumpet judgments seem to be focused on creation. These judgments affect the plants and animals, the water and air, and even God's greatest creation, people. One third is a prominent number in this series of judgments, and the reason is unclear. Perhaps God takes as much as He can without dooming the world entirely.

THE FIRST TRUMPET

The first plague is hail mixed with fire and blood. God is the One who sends this plague; it is not some ecological disaster that man creates for himself. This is true of all the plagues listed in the trumpet judgments. This hail and fire burns up one third of the trees and all of the green grass on earth. Can you imagine?

The smoke from the fire will fill the air all over the world. Plus, one third of the plants which help filter the air and produce oxygen will have been destroyed. What effect will that have on the ability to breath? Will the entire world become like a mountain region with less oxygen? Will the mountain regions become uninhabitable because of even less oxygen?

This plague could cause serious problems in many ways. The lack of oxygen will effect humans and animals. Working will be harder as you try to catch your breath. But, eventually the body will adjust. The animals who live on vegetation will have less food, if any. Cows need grass in order to produce milk, so dairy products will be in short supply until the grass returns. Animals that live in wooded areas may have to move to the city, literally. This plague sounds simple until you stop and think of the ramifications. Then it becomes very serious and scary.

THE SECOND TRUMPET

Something like a burning mountain falls to earth at the sounding of the second trumpet. This could be an asteroid, or a large meteor, or something God created just for this purpose. Whatever it is, it turns one third of the sea to blood, kills one third of the sea life, and destroys one third of the ships.

It is hard to imagine the stench that this would create. The dead sea life, rotting, would be a terrible odor, not to mention the blood. The people living near the ocean would have a terrible smell to deal with. The smell could spread all over the globe with that large of an area affected.

Food production would be greatly diminished with the first two trumpets. The first cut down the beef industry, along with other grass eating animals. The fire could have destroyed grains as well, but that is not known. The countries that rely on sea life for their food will now feel the effects of reduced availability. The shipping industry, which is how much of our food is transported between countries, will be crippled by the loss of one third of its fleet.

THE THIRD TRUMPET

John describes a star called Wormwood, falling to earth and polluting one third of the sources of fresh water. Obviously this is not a real star because stars are larger than the earth. However, it could be something that God creates which looks like a star and breaks up as it falls to earth, contaminating the fresh water supply. Wormwood is a plant that grows in Palestine, and has a strong, bitter taste. But, the plant is not poisonous. This star though will poison one third of the fresh water, making it unfit to drink.

The calamities are getting worse and worse. The main theme for the people of earth during this period is going to be survival. Where people were once striving to make that next dollar to afford a pool, a new car, or some other luxury, now they are just trying to find the basic need of fresh water. People can survive for an extended period of time without much food, but they cannot survive without water. People will drink the water, maybe out of desperation, and they will die.

THE FOURTH TRUMPET

God now steps up His attack against creation by moving out beyond the earth. With the blast of the fourth trumpet God causes one third of the sun, moon and stars to stop giving light. I do not understand exactly how He is going to do it, but He will cause the day to be one third shorter, and have total darkness, with no stars for one third of the night.

The way I see this happening is that God will work in sections. He will darken one third of the light coming from the sun in such a way that instead of having twelve hours of daylight, the earth will only have eight hours of daylight. It may be something like a partial eclipse, only darker. The same would be true for the stars. God would simply eclipse the light coming from one third of the night sky.

At any one time on earth it is summer in one hemisphere, and winter in another, except during the fall and spring seasons when the sunlight falls closer to the equator. Those in the summer regions would suddenly be cast into fall like conditions with the diminished sun. Those in winter regions would be in deep, almost polar, winter. If this plague strikes around the time of one of the equinoxes, the whole earth would be thrown into winter.

The diminished sunlight and heat from the sun would hurt the crops and plants. They would go prematurely dormant, or not grow at all. Once again, this will hurt the food supply. Fuel for the winter regions could be a problem as well. We are not told how long this plague will last, but it will surely be enough to do some damage, or it wouldn't be a plague.

Darkness is always associated with sin. It is said that most sin is done under cover of darkness. In his Gospel, John writes that men loved darkness more than light (John 3:19). They loved darkness because their actions were evil, and they wanted more darkness to be able to hide their actions. They did not want to give up their evil ways. With this trumpet judgment, God gives men what they want, more darkness.

It is also important to note here that it would be difficult for this plague to follow the sixth seal judgment. In the sixth seal, everything celestial is done away with in what would appear to be a permanent way. It is doubtful that God would restore everything back again, just to remove one third later. It is doubtful, but not impossible.

> At this point there is a break in the action as an angel comes out to warn people of the impending blasts from the other three trumpets. God is about to turn His attention, and punishment, onto His greatest creation, people.

THE FIFTH TRUMPET

Ok, so you're low on oxygen, you're low on food and water, it's darker and colder than you like it to be, and the whole world stinks (literally). So what else can happen? Well, the fifth angel gives a blast on his trumpet and four things happen.

The first thing John sees is a star falling to the earth. This is an obvious reference to an angelic being because it is followed by him receiving the key to the bottomless pit. Since this angel fell from heaven we can assume it is one of Satan's followers. Angels of God are usually referred to as being sent to earth, or going to earth, but rebellious angels are usually referred to as fallen.

This demon is then given the key to the bottomless pit. We believe this to be a reference to hell, where the soul/spirit of refusers are kept, as well as some of the fallen angels. But, this could also be something different, perhaps a special holding place for some things that are evil. The key is given to this angel by God, Who must be holding on to the keys, otherwise this coming terror would have been unleashed on the world earlier.

The third action to take place is the opening of the bottomless pit. This could just be a reference to the inside of the earth itself, which would basically be bottomless. This pit must be physically on the earth because the smoke fills the air of the earth. The already depleted oxygen is given another test, and the already diminished sun is blacked out for a while because of the smoke. Apparently the key the angel is given opens some fissure in the earth, releasing the smoke, much like a volcano, only worse.

The smoke was not the only thing released by this dark angel. The fourth action is locusts coming up out of the pit. These are not your ordinary, garden variety locusts. These guys are not going to eat grass and green stuff, God has already done enough on that front for now. These locusts are going to be like scorpions and they are going to hunt and hurt men.

They will sting people, and the pain will be like that of a scorpion sting. It is unclear whether the pain will last five months from a sting, or the locusts will only last five months. Either way it is bad for at least five months. [This is the only time we are given any kind of time frame for any of the plagues.] The pain from the sting will be so intense that people will want to die, but they can't. God is going to see to it that they feel the full effects of this judgment against them.

The locusts are going to go after people to hurt them, but they are not to hurt the people who have the mark of God on their foreheads. This means that the 144,000, and those accepters who are living at this time, will not suffer from these demonic locusts. Only those who have refused God will be tormented. This is the first time we have seen evidence that accepters are not going to suffer like everyone else. The other trumpet judgments have been generalized around the earth, and therefore the accepters would have some discomfort because of them. This plague is different because it is specific toward refusers. It also shows us that, although these creatures are demonic, they are still under the authority of God, and cannot go beyond the limits He has set. God is in absolute control of these judgments.

Did you notice the description John gives of these locusts? I believe he uses the words like or as at least eight times. They have what looks like armor plating, which is not unusual because grasshoppers look that way. They have what appear to be gold crowns on their heads. Their heads by the way are like a man's head, with a man's face. They have long hair, like a woman, but the teeth are like a lion's. Their breastplates are like iron, so it is doubtful you would be able to kill them by shooting them. Their wings make a rumbling sound like a herd of horses on the move. They have stingers on their scorpion-like tails.

Some people believe that John is simply trying to describe some weapon of modern warfare, such as a Cobra helicopter. But, that is highly improbable for several reasons. First, these beasts are seen to rise from the bottomless pit, which means they are not of earthly manufacture. Second, they are commanded not to hurt those with the mark of God on them. Weapons made by man would be indiscriminate in their targets. And, at this time especially, accepters would be targets of any weapon wielded by a man. Third, they have a supernatural, demonic king over them called Destroyer. He is the angel of the bottomless pit, probably the same one who was given the key to open it. Inanimate objects like helicopters cannot have a king, only the people driving them could. It just does not make sense that these creatures are anything but demonic locusts, who God allows to come up out of the pit to harm certain people, for a period of at least five months, because they have refused to accept God.

THE SIXTH TRUMPET

As if the demonic locusts were not bad enough, the sixth angel sounds his trumpet. Apparently there are four angels bound in the Euphrates River that runs from close to the Black Sea, through Turkey and Iraq, all the way to the Persian Gulf. These angels must be very dangerous if they are bound. Once again, these are probably fallen angels who followed Satan in his revolt against God. They are bound until a certain time that God already has planned out. God knows the exact hour when He is going to set these four angels free to kill one third of the remaining earth population.

Much has been made about the 200 million members of this army that is to be led by these angels. Who are they? The theories break down into three categories. These horsemen are either human beings, demons, or demon-possessed human beings.

Many people believe these to be human beings, or demon-possessed humans. It is said that China has a 200 million man army, or at least could have. Their national colors are red and yellow, which are the colors described by John on their breastplates. The fire, smoke and brimstone describe the gunpowder used in modern warfare, and invented by the Chinese. John could have been trying to describe tanks. By this theory, a Chinese army, with 200 million tanks, is going to take over a large area of the world, killing one third of the remaining population as they do so.

The remaining theory is that this is a supernatural army of demons, headed by these four angels. First, supernatural armies are mentioned in other places in the Bible. Elisha, in 2 Kings 6:14–17, saw an army of heavenly angels protecting him from the king's army of men. Joshua met the captain of the Lord's army near Jericho (Joshua 5:13–15). Revelation 19:14, speaks of the armies of heaven following Jesus at His return. These are all references to the army of angels who follow God. We see a demonic army in Revelation 12:7–8. Here, Satan and his army battle the army of God and lose. A demonic army of 200 million is not out of the question.

A second reason for believing this is a supernatural army is because of the description John gives of the horses. John describes them as horses, so they were apparently recognizable as horses. He did not use the terms "like" or "as" of them, even though he is careful to do so in the rest of his description of them. He says that the heads of the horses are like the head of a lion, and the tails are like serpents with heads. The fire, smoke and brimstone (sulfur) came from the mouth of the horse. The fire, smoke and sulfur killed people. The snake tails only hurt people. The text suggests that there were the same number of horses as members of the army, 200 million.

A third reason for believing this to be a supernatural army comes from extrapolation. This judgment occurs late in the tribulation period, at a time when Anti-Christ would have control of the earth. An army of 200 million killing off one third of the remaining population just does not make sense. Either this army would be under the control of Anti-Christ, or it would be a rogue army. What would be the point in Anti-Christ killing off one third of his people? If it is a rogue army, then why is no battle mentioned with an opposing army? The scripture seems to say that this army is unopposed in its killing. A human army of this size, at this time, with this mission, just does not make sense in relation to the rule of Anti-Christ.

A final reason for believing this is a supernatural army is the result that God was looking for in sending this judgment. Revelation 9:20–21 tells us that the people who were left did not stop their evil actions, or worshipping false gods. This was the point in letting this army loose. God wanted to show these people what Satan's army was capable of, and yet they did not turn to God. It was not about land, or even killing people, it was about getting people to turn to God.

People will continue to have varying opinions on this subject. I do believe that this massive army is a supernatural army. Like the locusts of the last judgment, they will be given restrictions as to what they can do, only one third of the population is killed, and perhaps they cannot kill accepters, although we are not told this. Satan wants people with him. If he can kill them before they come to God, he will do it. So, a Satanic army reaping souls for Satan is not too unbelievable. Whether it is human or supernatural, this army is going to kill one third of the remaining population of the earth, and that is a lot of dead people. This is a horrific judgment.

> John takes a break here to discuss a little scroll and the two witnesses. He also comments about the Seven Thunders. We do not know what these are. They could be another series of judgments, or they could be totally unrelated. If they are judgments, then there is a gap in our knowledge of what is going to happen during the tribulation. This makes it much harder to be sure of the series of events. It is important for us to remember that God has chosen not to disclose everything about this period.

THE SEVENTH TRUMPET

With the sounding of the seventh trumpet it appears we have once again reached the end of the tribulation period. There are voices in heaven declaring that the kingdoms of this world now belong to Jesus. This could only be true if Jesus were coming to conquer the earth by defeating Satan and Anti-Christ. The twenty-four elders declare that it is time for judgment of the Old Testament prophets and for the saints. This could be referring to the resurrection of the Old Testament saints, and the tribulation saints in preparation for their entrance into the millennial kingdom. The elders also call for the destruction of those who destroy the earth, this would be a purging of all refusers from the earth, just prior to the millennial kingdom (The sheep and goats judgment). We also see the temple of God opened and have various things happen which we will see again in the seventh bowl judgment.

All signs point to this trumpet being at the end of the tribulation. It is the preparation for Jesus taking the earth and making it His own to rule.

TRUMPET JUDGMENTS

TRUMPET	DESCRIPTION
ONE **REVELATION 8:7**	Hail and fire mingled with blood. 1/3 of trees burned. All green grass burned.
TWO **REVELATION 8:8–9**	Burning mountain cast into the sea. 1/3 of sea becomes blood. 1/3 of sea life dies. 1/3 of ships destroyed.
THREE **REVELATION 8:10–11**	Great star called Wormwood falls on 1/3 of the rivers and fountains of waters. 1/3 of the waters become wormwood and many men die because of the waters.
FOUR **REVELATION 8:12–13**	1/3 of the sun and moon darkened, and 1/3 of the stars darkened.
FIVE **REVELATION 9:1–12**	Angel opens bottomless pit and the sun and air are darkened with the smoke. Strange locusts, like scorpions, sting people and hurt them for five months. The king of the scorpions is the angel of the bottomless pit, Abaddon, or Apollyon.
SIX **REVELATION 9:13–21**	Supernatural army of 200 million is released to kill 1/3 of mankind.
SEVEN **REVELATION 11:15–19**	It is announced that the kingdoms of this world are now to be Christ's. The temple in heaven is opened. Lightnings, and voices, and thunderings, and an earthquake, and great hail.

THE BOWL JUDGMENTS

> **READ: REVELATION 16:1–21**

The seal judgments were about Anti-Christ and his kingdom, the trumpet judgments were against creation. The bowl judgments are against the refusers. In this set of judgments, God targets those who have refused to accept Him, even after all of these plagues, and chances He has given them to come to Him. There are seven angels who have seven bowls that contain the wrath of God. They are ordered by a voice from the temple, which is God, to go and pour out their bowls on the earth. The descriptions are short for each of the bowls, which may mean that they come in rapid succession. People may have very little time to recover from one judgment before being hit with another one.

THE FIRST BOWL

We know that the bowl judgments will not start until sometime after the 3 ½ year mark of the tribulation. The first bowl judgment is directed against those who have the mark of the beast, and this mark does not come into existence until after the mid-point of the tribulation. There will also have to be time allowed for people to receive the mark and make their decision whether to follow God or the Beast.

For those who accept the mark, God causes them to have a terrible sore. It is not certain what this sore is, but it is foul and evil. It could be a cancer, or it could be an ulcer. Whatever it is, it will not be pleasant, and it does not affect those without the mark of the beast.

THE SECOND BOWL

The second bowl touches the sea. In the second trumpet judgment one third of the sea was changed to blood. In this second bowl judgment, the entire sea is changed to blood. If they thought the problem was bad before, now it is terrible. All sea life dies because it cannot live in blood. And this stench will definitely encompass the entire planet. In other words, the beach will no longer be a fun vacation spot.

THE THIRD BOWL

The third trumpet polluted one third of the sources of fresh water, the third bowl will now turn all sources of fresh water into blood. This may be a temporary condition, or it may be close enough to the end of the tribulation that it remains until Jesus returns. If I remember my science correctly, a person can survive by drinking blood. It can hydrate you, not as well as water, but you can still survive.

The angel considers the turning water into blood pay-back for the refusers killing accepters. They spilled the blood of the followers of God, so let them drink blood. You can almost hear the souls we saw under the altar in the fifth seal cheering. According to the angel this judgment is directed against refusers who follow the Beast. It is unknown whether God will furnish accepters with water during this time.

THE FOURTH BOWL

The fourth trumpet cut off the light from one third of the sun; now God is going to make the sun hotter. Can you imagine? All you have is blood to drink, and now there is going to be unbearable heat? The people do understand Who is doing this to them. They curse God and refuse to accept Him as the true authority in the universe. They choose to continue following the Beast and relying on themselves. They refuse to allow God into their life, or to follow His rules.

THE FIFTH BOWL

Darkness now falls on the kingdom of the Beast. Exodus 10 gives us the account of some of the plagues God brought on Egypt in order to convince Pharaoh to let Israel leave. Verse 21 begins the telling of the darkness which filled the land of Egypt. It was a darkness that could be felt. No Egyptian was able to even move for three days, but those of Israel had light where they were. I believe this darkness of the fifth bowl will be something like that. This is darkness against the Beast and his followers, so they will suffer like the Egyptians. But the accepters will be able to see and have light.

This is going to be worse for those who follow the Beast than it was for the Egyptians. Revelation tells us that these people are in great pain, and suffering from their sores (probably the ones from the first bowl judgment). Imagine being in pain and not being able to see or move to reach your pain medication. These people are chewing on their tongues because of the pain.

And yet, we are reminded once again that these people will not turn from following the Beast. They will not ask God for forgiveness and accept Him into their life. Instead they just curse God for inflicting this pain on them. Meanwhile, the accepters are pain free and in the light.

THE SIXTH BOWL

Apparently the darkness is lifted. The Beast, the False Prophet, and Satan have had enough. They send out messengers to all the world telling them to gather their armies at the valley of Megiddo in Israel. These messengers can perform miracles, and they convince the leaders to send their armies.

The objective is to defeat this God who has been causing all of the trouble. Israel is God's special people, so the armies are going to threaten Israel and draw out their God for a fight with Him. The people are convinced they can win because they see the miracles the messengers perform, and because Satan is the father of all liars.

The blood must have changed back to water at some point because God dries up the water, not the blood, of the Euphrates River to aid these armies in their move to Megiddo. God is basically allowing these people to hang themselves, as we will see later. What transpires is referred to as the battle of Armageddon, and we will look at it after we look at the seventh bowl.

THE SEVENTH BOWL

As the armies of the world are moving toward Megiddo, the seventh bowl is poured out. This bowl has characteristics of both the sixth seal, and the seventh trumpet.

Like the seventh trumpet, there is a voice from the temple, lightning and voices and thunders. Hail stones weighing 100 pounds fall to the earth. The sixth seal, the seventh trumpet and the seventh bowl judgments all speak of a catastrophic, world-wide, earthquake that levels the mountains and destroys cities. Jerusalem will be divided into three parts with this earthquake.

Even up to the end, people are still going to curse God because He has brought all of this judgment on them. They do not realize that God has been doing this for their own good. He has given them mild punishments as a demonstration of His power and ability to punish. He wants them to realize that, if they think this is bad, try spending an eternity in the lake of fire without God. But these people made their decision to follow the Beast. They took his mark and would never turn away from it. They refused to accept God when He was giving them grace prior to the tribulation period, then they refused when He demonstrated His holiness during the tribulation. They can curse God all they want, it will not change the inevitable. They will spend an eternity in the lake of fire because that is what they chose when they refused God.

BOWL JUDGMENTS

BOWL   DESCRIPTION

ONE **REVELATION 16:2**	Sores on those with the mark of the beast.
TWO **REVELATION 16:3**	Sea becomes blood and all sea life dies.
THREE **REVELATION 16:4–7**	Rivers and sources of fresh water become blood.
FOUR **REVELATION 16:8–9**	Men scorched with extreme heat.
FIVE **REVELATION 16:10–11**	Darkness falls on the kingdom of the beast. Great pain and sores are suffered.
SIX **REVELATION 16:12–16**	Euphrates River dries up. The armies of the world begin to gather at Armageddon.
SEVEN **REVELATION 16:17–21**	Voice from the temple saying, "It is done." Lightning, voices, and thundering, and a great earthquake. Jerusalem is divided into three parts. Cities of the nations fall. Every Island and mountain leveled. 100 pound hailstones fall.

ARMAGEDDON

> **READ: REVELATION 19:11–21**

At the end of the tribulation period comes the battle of Armageddon. It is not a battle where all the nuclear capable countries of the world launch their warheads at each other, totally annihilating the planet earth. It is not even man versus man. This is man versus God, and it is not really much of a battle.

Satan gets all of the armies of the world gathered together in the valley of Megiddo. They are confident that they can beat God. Jesus comes from heaven on His white horse, with the armies of heaven following. Satan is captured and bound for 1,000 years, while the Beast and his False Prophet are captured and thrown into the lake of fire to spend eternity. At this point Jesus just speaks the word and everyone else in the army dies. John points out that the birds had a good feast. (When you think about it, the buzzards are probably the only ones who come out of the tribulation period well fed.)

THREE SEQUENCE CHARTS

There are three sequence charts people use in giving the sequence of events for the tribulation period. The most common chart is purely sequential. It looks something like this.

SEALS	TRUMPETS	BOWLS

This chart says that all seven seal judgments are completed then come the seven trumpet judgments. When they are finished, the bowl judgments begin. This is the most commonly held sequence chart today, and over the past centuries. However, this sequence has problems. First, it does not account for the seven thunders, if they are judgments.

Another problem is the fact that the seal judgments appear to go all the way through the tribulation period from beginning to end. We saw this evidenced by looking at Matthew 24. Also, the final trumpet and bowl judgments seem to be speaking of the same event as the sixth seal judgment.

The second sequence chart, which is not as well known, has all of the judgments running simultaneously.

| SEALS |
| TRUMPETS |
| BOWLS |

This sequence solves the problems of the first sequence. It allows for the seven thunders to also run, and it allows for the sixth seal, and seventh trumpet and bowl to be the same event. But it does run into a problem with the bowl judgments. We determined that the first bowl judgment could not start until after the 3 ½ year mark in the tribulation because it was against those with the mark of the beast. Therefore, the bowl judgments cannot start at the beginning of the tribulation period.

The final sequence chart has the judgments coming in staggered.

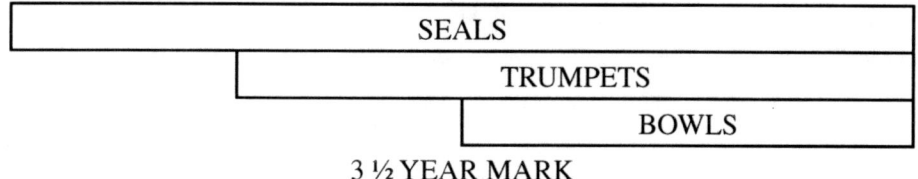

| SEALS |
| TRUMPETS |
| BOWLS |

3 ½ YEAR MARK

This sequence is almost unheard of, but it does solve the problems the other two present. It allows for the seven thunders, and it starts the bowl judgments after the 3 ½ year mark. It also has the judgments ending at the same time.

No one knows the time frame for each judgment, so the closest we can get is a sequence of events. Even that is not easy, especially if you use the last sequence chart.

John tells us in Revelation 10:8–11 about eating a little scroll. When he ate the scroll it was sweet in his mouth, but it was bitter in his stomach. That is the way it is when we study the tribulation period. We are glad that the bad people are finally getting theirs, but we are saddened by the fact that so many people will refuse God and end up in the lake of fire for eternity. The tribulation period will be the worst time in human history. We should never wish that anyone should have to experience it.

MIND THE GAP

You may think that the tribulation period is just about God having a lot of destructive fun, venting His pent-up anger. In reality, it is all about God giving refusers one more chance to turn to Him.

Compared to the infinite tortures of the eternal lake of fire, the tribulation disasters seem like a mild spanking. They are a little corporal punishment to keep people from suffering the greater pain.

God could have done two things. First, He could have just wiped everyone out all at once, giving no one a second chance. Second, He could have never warned us about what was to come. But, He did not do either of those things. He has warned us so that we can take care of the gap between us and Him today, instead of waiting until the punishments begin. Yet, even though we have been warned, He still makes provision for even more people to be able to come to Him during the tribulation.

There can be no doubt that God loves us and wants what is best for us. He does everything He can to get us into a good relationship with Him.

You're Outta Here!

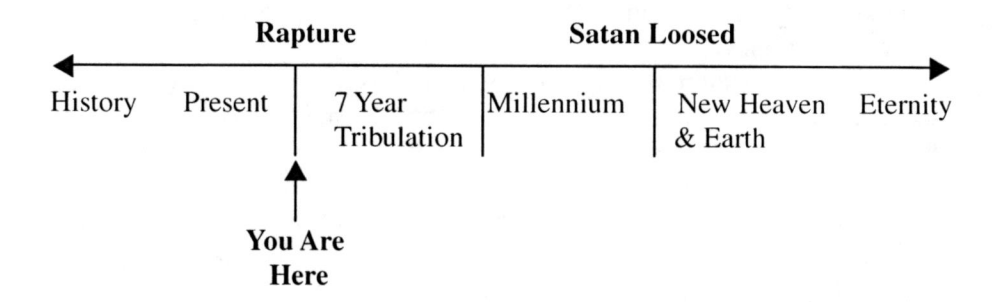

```
                Rapture           Satan Loosed
◄───────────────┬──────────┬──────────┬──────────────┬────────►
 History  Present │ 7 Year   │Millennium│ New Heaven   │ Eternity
                  │Tribulation│          │ & Earth      │
                  ▲
                  │
              You Are
               Here
```

Now we come to the most controversial event of the future, and the final event we will study. When we discussed the millennial kingdom, there was some controversy as to whether it would actually happen. With this next event the controversy is more centered on when it will occur. We will look at this event, what scripture has to say about when it will occur, and then how the three views for the timing of this event match up with scripture.

> **READ:** JOHN 14:1–3, 16–18, 26 AND 1 CORINTHIANS 15:51–57 AND 1 THESSALONIANS 4:13–17

As Jesus eats His final Passover meal with His disciples, He notices the mood is very solemn, and the disciples are upset. Jesus has been speaking to them about His impending death and resurrection, but they do not understand. All they know is that Jesus is going to leave them. Their hopes and dreams for the future kingdom are not going to be realized. They also love Jesus, and do not want to see Him leave.

Jesus begins to tell the disciples more about His future, and theirs. He tells them that He is going back to heaven to be with the Father. In heaven there are many places where people can live. Many translations say that there are many mansions in heaven, but the correct translation of the Greek word is dwelling. Jesus tells the disciples that He is going to prepare a place for them in heaven. He is going to make a spot for them to live in heaven. This is a promise from Jesus to His disciples. If it were not true, He would not have said anything to them about it. He is the Son of God, and anything He wants for His followers, He will get. Jesus can make all the living space He wants in heaven for those who love Him.

This promise sets up the next. Jesus tells His disciples that He will personally come for them, to take them to heaven to live in this space He has created for them, and to live with Him. This promise is not just to the eleven men eating with Jesus that night, it is for all who love Jesus, and have accepted Him into their life. Jesus is coming back some day to take those who love Him to heaven, to be with Him. His coming for the accepters is called the rapture, and it is what we will be looking at in this chapter.

Jesus goes on to make another promise during the meal. The disciples understand that He is going to come back for them, but what about the time when He is gone? Jesus knows their thoughts, and sees that they are upset about Him being away from them. He promises to send a Comforter to them. This Person would be with them, and live within them, while Jesus was away.

He would take the place of Jesus on this earth. The Comforter is the Holy Spirit, and He comes to live in the lives of accepters. His mission is to teach accepters about Jesus, and the Father, and about their ways. He helps us know how to live and do what is right. The Holy Spirit convinces people, even refusers, that there is such a thing as sin. He also helps to convince people that there is something good called righteousness, which is doing what is right. And, He convinces people that there are consequences to their bad actions. He is God within us, and is now God's physical presence on the earth. Once the Holy Spirit has entered into us, He will never leave.

This discussion by Jesus with His disciples goes beyond prophecy. He is not just predicting some future event. This is a personal promise by Jesus to return for those He loves, and who love Him. We see the heart of Jesus looking out for His people by making sure they will always have His presence in their life. By sending the Holy Spirit to live within them, Jesus provided a way for all of the accepters to know His personal teaching for their individual life, and to know His love in their life first hand. And, the Holy Spirit helps to bring more people to the point of accepting a relationship with Jesus.

When Jesus returns He will only be taking those who have a relationship with Him. There will be a sorting, and those who have refused Jesus will remain on the earth, while the accepters, who have the Holy Spirit, go to be with Him. The sorting should be simple enough. Jesus only takes those with the Holy Spirit.

This simple understanding, that Jesus is coming back for His own, led to some questions by the early church. What about those accepters who were already dead? Were the only ones who would experience this return be alive and the dead just miss out? How is this going to take place? What will happen to the accepters when this takes place? These are questions that the Apostle Paul tried to answer in some of his writings to the churches of Corinth and Thessalonica.

The Thessalonians had the question for Paul about those accepters who were already dead. Some may have been teaching that if a person dies before Jesus returns, they would lose any hope of being with Jesus in His kingdom. Paul wanted to make sure that this kind of false teaching did not spread. He tells them plainly what will happen when Jesus returns.

First, he reminds the readers that Jesus died and rose again, and so will all who have accepted Jesus. Then he tells them that Jesus will personally come down from heaven to meet people in the air. At this time Jesus will not be coming to the earth, only to the clouds, to retrieve His people. Paul goes on to say that the dead in Christ will rise first, then those who are still alive will be caught up to be with Him.

We get a broader picture when we include the statements Paul made to the Corinthians. Here Paul says that we will all be changed. We will go from this body which deteriorates, to one that will never wear out. We will be transformed from this body ravaged by sin, to a perfect, sinless body fit for heaven. In other words, we will become like the body Jesus has now. Those who have died will have this new improved body reunited with their soul, which has been in heaven since they died. Those who are alive will just find their bodies changed instantly.

We need to be clear on this point. The body we have now is not left behind in a heap like a snake's skin; it is changed. We keep the same body we have now, but God instantly makes the needed modifications to make it fit for heaven dwelling. How God is able to accomplish this with bodies which have been decayed for centuries, I do not have a clue. But, that is why He is God. He can, and will, do it.

How are we to be taken? Jesus personally calls for the accepters. The order from 1 Thessalonians is that the dead rise first, get their improved bodies, then the living get their bodies changed. Paul says that this will all take place in an instant, faster than we can blink our eye. One second we are living our life on earth, the next we are standing with Jesus in the clouds. From that moment on, we will always be with Jesus.

The word "rapture" is used to describe this event, but it is not found in the Bible. It comes from the Latin word for catching up, or snatching up. But, the Bible was not originally written in Latin, it was written in Greek. The Greek word Paul uses is ́arpozw (harpodzo) which is translated "caught up" in 1 Thessalonians 4:17. Doing a word study we find that this word is translated as *caught away, caught up, take it by force, pluck,* and *pulling.* In other Greek literature it is used with the idea of *snatching, seizing, taking something suddenly and vehemently.* It is also translated with the idea of *grasping something quickly, eagerly, and with desire.*

> **The rapture is the deliberate, forceful act of Jesus whereby He eagerly and with desire grasps those who are His, both dead and alive, snatching them from this world to be with Him forever.**

When we grasp the real meaning behind this word we can no longer think of Jesus just sitting in heaven passively waiting for the time to come get us.

The picture we get is of Jesus, more excited than a child waiting for Christmas to come, ready to return to get His people. Jesus will not just casually come either. He is both deliberate and forceful in His action. He will not just take his people from the earth; He will snatch them, greedily, to Himself. Accepters, Christians, are His prize possessions, and He does not want to be without them any longer than is necessary. Jesus can hardly wait for God the Father to give the command to go because He loves us so much. Jesus' whole desire and motivation is to have you with Him forever. If you have accepted Jesus into your life, you cannot help but smile when you think of Him loving you that much.

Now that we know what the rapture is, we come to the big question of when. What does scripture have to say about the timing of the rapture, especially in relation to other future events?

Matthew 24:36 finds Jesus in the middle of His discourse about the end times. Here He tells us that only God the Father knows when Jesus will be coming to get His own. The following passages tell us to be ready for this event. By this point in His speech, Jesus has already run through the entire tribulation scenario for His disciples. They know that there will be a time of tribulation, then Jesus will return to earth to set up His kingdom. So, if Jesus is speaking about when He comes to set up His kingdom, then the description of His coming in verses 36 through 39 will not make sense. There will really be no surprise to the people on earth that Jesus is coming at the end of the tribulation. Armies are massing at Megiddo, and the sign of the Son will appear in heaven (Matthew 24:30).

Jesus is obviously speaking of another coming, which He will make, in verses 36 through 39. This would be His coming for those who have accepted Him. This coming will be a surprise, unannounced to the world. We saw in 1 Thessalonians that He will be in the air, and all the accepters meet Him there. Those on earth never see Him. All they know is that people are now missing who were there just a second ago. People will be going about their daily lives, just like they did before the flood in Noah's time, and all of a sudden, people will be gone. Jesus will have come and they will have missed it. Only God knows when this is going to happen, and He isn't telling. It will definitely be an unexpected event, even to those who will be raptured.

**The rapture will be a surprise event. Only God knows its timing.
(Matthew 24:26–25:13)**

Paul had to write another letter to the Thessalonians. Apparently there were some people there spreading the lie that Jesus had already returned and they had missed it. Paul puts an end to this foolishness in 2 Thessalonians 2:1–12. He begins by splitting the Second Coming of Jesus into two events. One event is His coming to earth to set up His kingdom, and the other is His coming to gather the accepters to be with Him (the rapture).

Paul tells the people in verses 2 through 4 that Jesus will not come to set up His kingdom until after the man of sin (Anti-Christ) is revealed for who he really is. He uses the focal point of Anti-Christ's rule, his desecrating the temple in Jerusalem by setting himself up as God. This takes place at the 3½year mark of the tribulation.

According to verses 5 through 8, this man of sin, or lawlessness, cannot come to power until the One Who holds back lawlessness is taken out of the way. This begs the question, who holds back lawlessness? There are really only three possibilities: Satan, man, or God.

Satan would never hold back lawlessness because he causes it. Also, Satan is not removed from the earth before the Beast takes power. Anti-Christ actually gets his power from Satan. Removing Satan from the scene so that the Anti-Christ could take power would make no sense.

What about man, people? Since Adam and Eve mankind has had a sinful, lawless nature. We make laws to try to control this nature, but we really do not have much effect. If people want to break the law they do. Man is just not able to hold back lawlessness when it wants to exert itself. Besides, people are still on the earth when Anti-Christ comes to power, and Paul says that the restraint is removed so Anti-Christ can come to power. It is people who worship him as being God. It is not people who are keeping the Anti-Christ from being revealed and coming to power, they will welcome him.

God is the only one left. We know that God is holy and that His holiness makes Him absolutely against sin and lawlessness. Yet, He allows sin in this world because He has given us free will. God is powerful enough though to resist and restrain lawlessness when He wants. His presence holds back a lot of bad actions by people.

So, if God's presence holds back, or restrains, lawlessness and sin, then where is His presence in this world that is holding back the revealing of this man of sin? When Jesus left this earth He sent His Holy Spirit into the world to be His presence in the world. The Holy Spirit lives inside each and every accepter of Jesus. This is God's presence in the world today. He is the One Who moves in the hearts and lives of His people to resist the evil in their lives and in this world.

When Paul speaks of this One who resists evil and lawlessness being taken out of the world, he is speaking of God physically removing His presence from this earth. How would that be possible? God would have to take all of the accepters, who have the Holy Spirit within them, out of this world at one time. Face it, without the Christian resistance, the evil in this world will run rampant. Anti-Christ will never be able to come to power with a Christian resistance still in place.

Paul follows up on these thoughts in verses 9 through 12. He tells how God is going to give people a chance by telling them the truth about His love. This will come through the two witnesses and the 144,000. Many people will believe, but many more will refuse God. At a certain point people will refuse God and He will allow them to believe whatever they want. These people will follow the lies of the Anti-Christ; they will take the mark of the beast, and will suffer the consequences for eternity.

The influence of the Holy Spirit residing in accepters must be removed before the Anti-Christ can come to power. His rise to power actually begins before the tribulation period. We know that the seven years does not begin until the treaty between Israel and Anti-Christ is signed. Paul uses the desecration of the temple with Anti-Christ setting himself up as God as the sign that will reveal Anti-Christ to the world. Accepters would know this man at the signing of the treaty.

> **The influence of the Holy Spirit residing in accepters must be removed before the man of sin can come to power. (2 Thessalonians 2:3–12)**

Now let us return to Revelation 7:1–8. Here we find the sealing of the 144,000 servants of God. We brought up this point at the time, but it needs to be looked at again here. Only Jews are sealed as being servants of God. This event is prior to the tribulation judgments. We again raise the question, why were there not any non-Jewish people considered servants of God? Where is the church, the followers of Jesus who are predominately not Jewish? The fact that only Jews are sealed as servants of God suggests that all the other accepters have been taken out of this world.

The sequence could be something like this. The rapture occurs taking all of the Christians out of this world to be with Jesus. The two witnesses assigned by God come on the scene proclaiming their message. 144,000 Jews accept Jesus as their Messiah (Savior) because of this teaching. These 144,000 are then sealed by God to be witnesses for Him during the tribulation period. Through their witnessing, many people come into a relationship with Jesus.

It would seem unfair of God to only consider 144,000 Jewish people to be His servants when so many others have proven themselves as such throughout the ages. Those who have the Holy Spirit within them have a relationship with God, and they are servants of God without regard to nationality. So, when God only seals 144,000 men of one nationality, something drastic has changed in His relation to the world. Those who have His spirit within them must have been removed at some point because God could never turn His back on His own people like that.

> **The 144,000 Jews are the only servants of God sealed prior to the tribulation judgments.**
> **(Revelation 7:1–8)**

The tribulation period appears to be God's judgment on refusers. As we looked at the judgments during the tribulation period we noticed that many were directed toward refusers. 2 Thessalonians 2:10–12 seems to suggest that God has designed the tribulation period for refusers, to show them the truth about Himself, and for their punishment.

Paul stated in Romans 8:1 that those who have accepted Jesus as the payment for their sin do not suffer the same punishment, or condemnation, for sin that refusers suffer. God is not going to expose those who are in Him to the same punishment that He gives to those who refuse Him. The tribulation period is punishment for the continuing sin, or evil, of the refusers and their leader, Satan.

> **The tribulation period is God's judgment on refusers.**
> **(Romans 8:1 and 2 Thessalonians 2:10–12)**

The final thing we need to consider when looking at what scripture has to say about when the rapture will occur is something scripture is silent about. After John is given the messages to the churches in Revelation chapters 2 and 3, the church is never mentioned again. All through the showing of the events of the tribulation period, the church does not appear. The word saints appears, but the congregation of worldwide believers known as the church is not mentioned. This silence is unthinkable if the church is still in existence during the tribulation, especially when such an emphasis was placed on the church during the two chapters preceding the description of these events. You would think that God would have given people some idea of what is happening to the church and what their response should be to the events, if they were still there. Instead we are left with silence.

> **The church is no longer mentioned after Revelation 3.**

Three Theories on When the Rapture Will Take Place

There are three different times people believe the rapture could take place. All three are in relation to the tribulation period. We will look at each of these theories and compare them with what we have learned in scripture to see how they stack up.

POST-TRIBULATION RAPTURE

This theory says that the rapture will occur after the tribulation period. As Jesus is coming to fight the battle of Armageddon He will call for His people to come up to Him so they will not be hurt during the battle. This leaves only refusers on the earth for God to destroy. This sounds good, and practical, and it even matches up with meeting Jesus in the air. But it does not fare as well with the rest of scripture.

First, it would not be the surprise Jesus talked about in Matthew. Second, it does not deal with the problem of God's presence being taken away before Anti-Christ is revealed. Third, it does not account for 144,000 Jews being the only servants of God at the beginning of the tribulation. Fourth, it would mean that God is sending His judgment on the church as well as on refusers. Finally, it does not account for the silence of Revelation concerning the church during this time. Revelation is even silent about this event happening at the battle of Armageddon, even though it is graphic in other details.

I do not believe this theory meets the test of scripture.

MID-TRIBULATION RAPTURE

This theory says that the rapture will occur at the mid-point of the tribulation period, the 3½ year mark. Just prior to the revealing of the Anti-Christ and the crack down against accepters, the Christians will be pulled out of this world to be with Jesus, leaving the last half of the tribulation for the refusers only.

This could certainly fit with the Holy Spirit being removed before the revealing of the Anti-Christ, or at least before Anti-Christ sets himself up as God. And we could say that it fits with the great tribulation being the judgments on the refusers, if we considered the bowl judgments to be the true judgments against refusers.

However, this theory does not account for the surprise factor Jesus promised. People will know that the plagues have started and that Jesus would be returning before 3 ½ years have passed. Plus, by signing the treaty with Israel, Anti-Christ has already revealed himself, at least to accepters. It does not account for the 144,000 at the beginning of the tribulation, nor does it account for the silence about the church.

Another problem is the great multitude of people martyred during the tribulation period. The killing of the followers of God does not begin until the middle of the tribulation. There would not be enough time to rebuild a large following of Jesus in order to have that many people killed. Also, if all the accepters were taken in the middle of the tribulation, there would be no one left to witness for Jesus. The two witnesses would be gone, and the 144,000 would be raptured with the rest of the accepters. There would not be one person left on earth for Anti-Christ to kill as a follower of Jesus.

I do not believe this theory meets the test of scripture.

PRE-TRIBULATION RAPTURE

Those who hold to the pre-tribulation rapture theory believe that Jesus will come and take His own out of the world before the seven-year tribulation begins. This means that the next major event to occur in our study of future events is the rapture. It starts the whole process off.

The rapture will definitely be a surprise as people are going about their lives, not expecting it to happen at any moment. The Holy Spirit will be pulled out of the earth before Anti-Christ begins to put his power base together and sign the treaty with Israel. The 144,000 Jewish accepters of Jesus will begin evangelizing the earth for the great multitude of accepters who come out of the tribulation period. The tribulation period will be against those who refused Jesus up until the time He came to take His own home with Him, even though they become accepters during the tribulation. The church is no longer mentioned in Revelation because it is with Jesus in heaven. The new believers are to be known as tribulation saints, a completely distinct designation.

I believe this theory meets the test of scripture.

```
    PRE         MID        POST
     ↑           ↑           ↑
     |           |           |
    T R I B U L A T I O N   P E R I O D
```

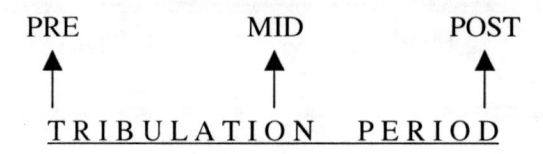

What should we learn from our study of the rapture? When it is going to happen is not the most important thing. First and foremost, we must learn that Jesus loves each of us very much. It is His primary desire and motivation that each person who has accepted Him into their life be with Him. He anxiously awaits the day when the Father will tell Him that it is time to come get us.

We must be ready, or we will be left to suffer the judgments of the tribulation period. If you have never accepted Jesus into your life as the payment for your sin, then you are not ready. Those who have accepted Jesus have the Holy Spirit within them. They are the ones who will be taken. Not only should we be ready, but we must do what we can to see that others are ready too. We should not keep the information we have about God's love and holiness to ourselves, we must share.

God knows each person intimately. He knows if you have really accepted Him into your life or not. We can fool ourselves into thinking we have that relationship, but we cannot fool God. If we are truly relying on Jesus to get us to heaven, and not on church membership or the good things we do, then we are God's, and we have the Holy Spirit within us. As Jesus winds up His sermon in Matthew 7, he tells us that not everyone who calls Him Lord, will enter into heaven. Some will deceive themselves into thinking they are going to heaven, but they never had a relationship with Jesus. We must be sure of where we stand with God, and why, or we may miss the rapture.

Paul wrote to Titus (2:11–14) that the rapture is our blessed hope. It is what we look forward to. We will be transported from this world, and be with Jesus for eternity. Peter tells us in his letter that this should make us want to live holy lives (2 Peter 3, especially verses 11 and 14). As we live in hope for our future translation to Jesus, we should want to live holy lives so He does not find us doing something of which He would not approve. Jesus always stressed that people live lives that would be ready to go at any time, without embarrassment.

THE JUDGMENT SEAT OF CHRIST

> **READ**: ROMANS 14:10–12 AND 2 CORINTHIANS 5:10 AND 1 CORINTHIANS 3:10–15

The final future event we need to look at is the Judgment Seat of Christ. We have seen the judgment of the refusers at the Great White Throne judgment, and the judgment concerning who enters the millennial kingdom with the Judgment of the Nations (sorting of the sheep and the goats.) Now we are going to look at the judgment of the accepters before God.

Romans 14:10–12 tells us that every single person in the world will stand before God to be judged. Accepters are not immune from this. Paul is writing these words to the church of Rome to let them know that their thoughts and actions do matter to God. He says that those who have a relationship with Jesus will stand before the Judgment Seat of Christ.

Paul tells the Corinthian church in his second letter to them, that accepters will all stand before Jesus to give an accounting of their work on earth. Jesus will judge these works to be good or bad. But Paul was just summarizing what he had already told the Corinthians in his first letter to them about the judgment accepters will receive.

Using the illustration of a builder, Paul relates how each of us builds our life work. Some of the works we do are very good, and are like building with gold and silver. Other things we do are bad, and are like building with wood, and straw. God will judge our works with fire, and those made of metal, that will not burn, will be saved. However, the bad works that were made of straw and wood will be lost.

The important thing to remember about the passage in 1 Corinthians is the foundation. No matter what, the foundation cannot be burned or lost. The foundation is Jesus, and the work He has already done for us in paying for our sin. Our eternal place with God in heaven is secure; nothing can take that away from us. It is the work we have done after accepting Jesus into our life that will be judged.

Not only will our actions be judged, but our motives as well. Jesus knows what we are thinking. He knows if we gave money to a charity just so people will make a big deal over us, or notice us. He also knows those times when we do some selfless act that no one else sees. If our motive in doing something is to make us look good, then that action, no matter how good, will be burned.

But, if our motive is to truly help people, or honor God, then that will stand the fire.

The worthless actions that we have done will be destroyed, but the good ones will be left. The foundation never moves. This is different than the Great White Throne judgment. There, people are judged by their works to see if they can enter heaven. Of course, none of their works are good enough, because only the work of Jesus is good enough to get anyone into heaven. An accepter's eternal destiny is not on the line, just the amount of reward they will receive from God.

This judgment will come after the rapture of the church. It is not clear when, but it will be after that rapture. All of the accepters who have lived since Jesus will be judged at this time. All of the Old Testament saints and Tribulation saints will be judged at the Judgment of Nations, just prior to the millennium. And all of the refusers of God, from all of the ages, will be judged at the Great White Throne judgment. While we should look forward to it with some fear, we should want to be a part of the Judgment Seat of Christ.

Every time I teach on this subject I am asked the question, "What about the children? Are they raptured, or left behind?" In all honesty, I do not know. I can find no scripture, which is definitive on the subject, and so I am hesitant to give a definite answer. However, I will say this. I believe God will do what is right. Remember that God is holy, so He will always do what is right. If it is right for Him to take the children to be with Him at the time of the rapture, He will. If it is not right, then He will leave them.

To come to any other conclusion than to just trust God would be difficult, as well as detrimental. We could banter around for years about ages, and the ability to understand, in order to make some type of formula for which child would stay and which would be taken. Let us leave it up to God. And let's make sure our children are prepared to go by helping them enter into a relationship with Jesus as soon as they are able to understand what that means.

Relying on God to make the right decision also applies to those who are not mentally capable of understanding about Jesus. This is not avoiding the issue; it is understanding our limitations on the matter, and God's perfection in doing what is right, just, and fair. God loves us, especially the children and those who are never able to be more than children in their understanding. He will do what is best for them, with love.

MIND THE GAP

I know there are people reading this book who have lived through, or are living through, abuse and loneliness. All your life people have used you to further their own ends. You have never known someone who really loves you and cares about you. So, when you come to the definition of the rapture, it is very hard for you to connect with that concept. To think that someone actually loves you so much that they cannot wait to be with you.

And yet, the Bible clearly tells us that Jesus loves us. The God who created this universe loves us enough that He made a huge sacrifice, just so we could be with Him for eternity (John 3:16).

God, Jesus, wants to be with you because He loves you. There is nothing special about us that makes God want to be with us, or to love us. He simply chooses to do it. He sacrificed everything just to have a chance at a relationship with you and me. Let that sink in. Someone actually does love you, with no ulterior motives, simply because He chooses to love you. And He cannot wait for the day the two of you can stand face to face and spend an unlimited amount of time together. His strongest desire is for you to be with Him.

The rapture will be a surprise, which means we have no idea when it will occur. This should give immediacy to our actions. As accepters we must make sure that refusers know the truth about what is coming for them. Accepters must also learn to feel the love God has for them, and then share that love with those around them. For refusers, they must accept what God has done for them because of His love for them. All of this must be done like there is no tomorrow.

When
It's All
Been
Said And
Done

We have looked at a lot of material from the Bible; scriptures about people and events that are yet to come to this world and its inhabitants. But, we have really been looking at them in reverse. So, at this time, let me kind of run the events again, in the order that I believe they will occur.

REVIEW OF THE EVENTS

The very next big event as far as Bible prophecy is concerned is the rapture. Millions of people all over the world will disappear in an instant, without warning. The dead who have a relationship with Jesus will be resurrected, and those accepters who are still alive will just have their bodies changed. All of these people will meet Jesus in the air, and will be judged at the Judgment Seat of Christ.

Following the rapture will come the tribulation period. It is not reaching too far to believe that the worldwide event of the rapture will force the world to call for a world leader to rise up and take charge. The Anti-Christ (the Beast) will rise to prominence on the world stage, leading his ten-member confederation. The seven-year clock begins to tick when the treaty of protection is signed between Israel and the Anti-Christ. This seven-year period will see many devastating plagues sent by God against those who refuse to follow Him.

Just prior to the actual tribulation period, God will seal 144,000 Jews as His servants. These men will have accepted Jesus into their life after the rapture, and they will be used to spread the news about God during the tribulation. The two witnesses, who will boldly proclaim the message of God to the nations from the temple in Jerusalem, will aid them during the first half of the tribulation. These two men will have great power to perform miracles. Anyone who wants to hurt them will be killed by fire coming out of their mouth.

After 3 ½ years, Anti-Christ is able to kill the two witnesses. He breaks his protection treaty with Israel and sets himself up as God in the temple in Jerusalem. He then begins to persecute those of Israel, and those who follow Jesus. His head henchman, the False Prophet, institutes a mark of loyalty known as the mark of the beast. Those without this mark will not be able to buy or sell anything, and will be killed. Many accepters will die during this time.

At the end of the horrible tribulation period, Jesus returns to fight the battle of Armageddon. It is not much of a battle as Jesus wins easily. He then sets up His kingdom on earth. For 1,000 years Satan is bound and cannot deceive anyone, or tempt them into sinning. But, after the thousand years is over, God releases Satan for a little while. He convinces people to follow him, and raises an army to go against God. This army is summarily wiped out by fire from heaven, and Satan is cast into the lake of fire.

All refusers, face the Great White Throne judgment. All of these people are cast into the lake of fire to spend their eternity without God, which is the same way each one of them wanted to live their life. Accepters though, get to spend their eternity with Jesus in a new heaven and a new earth.

All The Way From Kingdom Come

	ONE	TWO	THREE	FOUR	FIVE	SIX	SEVEN
SEALS	Rev. 6:1–2 Mt. 24:6 Zech. 1:8–11 6:3–6, 8	Rev. 6:3–4 Mt. 24:7a Zech. 1:8–11 6:2–5	Rev. 6:5–6 Mt. 24:7b Zech. 6:2–8	Rev. 6:7–8 Mt. 24:7b Zech. 1:8–11 6:3–7 I Chron. 21:14–27	Rev. 6:9–11 Mt. 24:9–28	Rev. 6:12–17 Mt. 24:29–31 Isa. 2:19–21 13:10 24:19–23 34:4 Joel 2:31 3:15	Rev. 8:1

	ONE	TWO	THREE	FOUR	FIVE	SIX	SEVEN
TRUMPETS	Rev. 8:7	Rev. 8:8–9	Rev. 8:10–11	Rev. 8:12–13	Rev. 9:1–12	Rev. 9:13–21	Rev. 11:15–19

	ONE	TWO	THREE	FOUR	FIVE	SIX	SEVEN
BOWLS	Rev. 16:2	Rev. 16:3	Rev. 16:4–7	Rev. 16:8–9	Rev. 16:10–11	Rev. 16:12–16	Rev. 16:17–21

TWO WITNESSES: Killed by Beast and ascend — Rev. 11:1–14

TRAMPLING OF THE HOLY CITY (JERUSALEM) BY GENTILES

Treaty with Anti-Christ	ISRAEL Treaty Broken Satan Cast From Heaven? Abomination of Desolation Dan. 12:11	Rev. 12:6, 13–17 Mt. 24:15–21 IN HIDING
3 ½ YEARS		3 ½ YEARS

144,000 Sealed (Revelation 7:1–8)

Satan Cast From Heaven? (Revelation 12:7–12)

Rapture (Revelation 14:14–16)

Christ Returns (Revelation 19:11–21) / Battle of Armageddon (Joel 3:9–17; (Rev. 14:17–20, 19:17–21)

1,000 Years of Millennial Reign (Revelation 20:1–6)

Satan Loosed and Doomed (Rev. 20:7–10) / Great White Throne Judgment (Rev. 20:11–15)

New Heaven and New Earth (Revelation 21:1–22:5)

REVIEW OF THE DEAD

Another aspect of future events, which we mention, is the dead. I have tried to chart the path of the dead concerning where the bodies are, where the souls are kept, and which judgments they face. This is not a morbid curiosity. It is important to understanding the future everyone faces.

As it stands now, in today's pre-rapture world, the dead bodies of everyone are on earth. They are either buried on land, or in the water. The soul/spirit of an accepter is in the temporary holding place in heaven with God. The soul/spirit of the refuser is in Hades (Hell), the temporary holding place.

When the rapture occurs, the bodies of the dead accepters will be rejoined with their soul/spirit. Those accepters who are alive will be changed and taken up to heaven. At this point the body and soul/spirit of every accepter is in heaven with God. None of their bodies are left on earth. All of the accepters face the Judgment Seat of Christ.

The bodies of refusers remain on earth during the tribulation period. Other bodies of accepters, the tribulation saints, will be added to them. The soul/spirit of a tribulation saint will go immediately to heaven at death. The soul/spirit of a refuser will still go to Hades.

When Jesus returns to earth, He will resurrect the bodies of the Old Testament saints, and the Tribulation saints, and join them with their soul/spirit. These people will now live with Jesus in the millennial kingdom, along with the other accepters. Jesus will also hold a Judgment of Nations. Those who are refusers will be killed and their soul/spirit sent to Hades. Their bodies will remain on earth. There will still be people who are accepters, who are alive on the earth during this time.

After the Millennium Satan is loosed, and the final battle is won by God. At that time the body and soul/spirit of all accepters will be placed in the new heaven and earth to live for eternity. At the Great White Throne judgment, all of the bodies of the refusers will be resurrected to be joined with their soul/spirit. They will be judged and cast into the lake of fire to spend eternity.

This is the path that is taken by our bodies and our soul/spirit. The path taken depends on whether we accept Jesus into our life or not.

114 All The Way From Kingdom Come

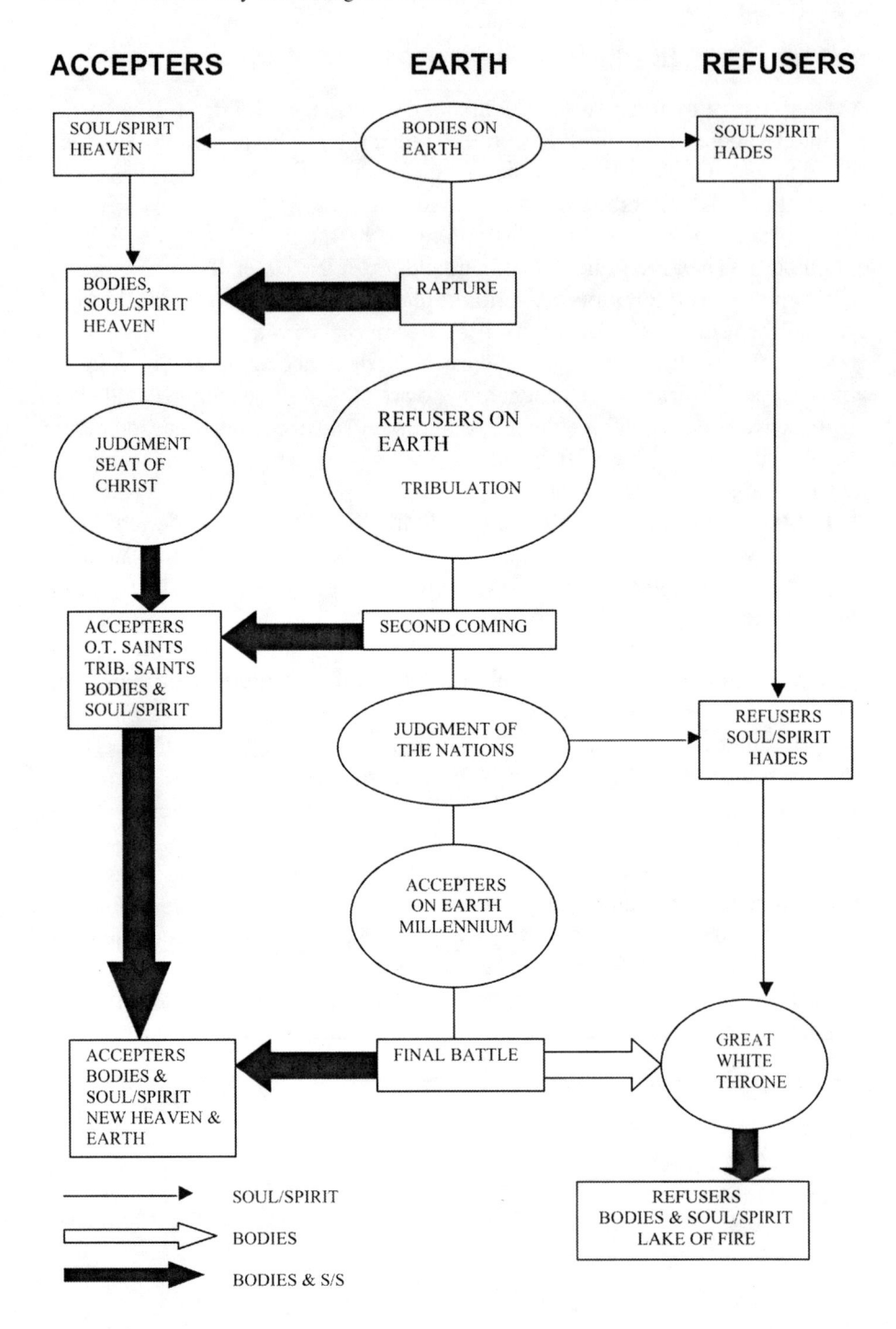

ACCEPTERS EARTH REFUSERS

```
SOUL/SPIRIT     ← BODIES ON  →  SOUL/SPIRIT
HEAVEN            EARTH           HADES

BODIES,         ← RAPTURE
SOUL/SPIRIT
HEAVEN

                  REFUSERS ON
JUDGMENT          EARTH
SEAT OF
CHRIST            TRIBULATION

ACCEPTERS       ← SECOND COMING
O.T. SAINTS
TRIB. SAINTS
BODIES &
SOUL/SPIRIT
                  JUDGMENT OF   →  REFUSERS
                  THE NATIONS       SOUL/SPIRIT
                                    HADES
                  ACCEPTERS
                  ON EARTH
                  MILLENNIUM

ACCEPTERS       ← FINAL BATTLE  ⇒  GREAT
BODIES &                            WHITE
SOUL/SPIRIT                         THRONE
NEW HEAVEN &
EARTH
                                  REFUSERS
                                  BODIES & SOUL/SPIRIT
                                  LAKE OF FIRE
```

→ SOUL/SPIRIT
⇒ BODIES (outline arrow)
➡ BODIES & S/S (solid arrow)

What Should We Take From This?

Studying future events should have more of an impact on us than just learning facts about what is to come. It should have an effect on other areas of our life, and it can give us insight into how we view certain things. In this final section, I just want us to go through each section we studied and look at some important thoughts and insights we need to take away from them.

NEW HEAVEN AND EARTH

Seeing where people are going to spend eternity because of their choice concerning God should motivate us to spread the gospel. It should motivate us through fear. We should be afraid for those who refuse God, and want to see them turned from the direction they are heading. We should not want to see anyone spend an eternity in the lake of fire. And, it should motivate us through love. We should love others enough to want them to spend an eternity in heaven, with Jesus. We should love Jesus enough to want to share Him with others. We have the answer for the eternal destiny of everyone in this world. We must share it, or it will not be known.

Seeing into eternity helps us to put the here-and-now into perspective. When measured against eternity, many of our every-day problems seem petty. Much of what we work for, and strive for, seems unimportant. Our priorities begin to look different as we move our relationship with God to the top of the list. When we live with eternity in mind, it will make the here-and-now seem less traumatic.

MILLENNIUM

It may not seem like much in the whole scheme of things, but how you deal with the millennium issue is very important. It helps bring to light how you handle the scriptures. Do you allow the truth of the scripture to reveal itself to you? Or, do you come to the Bible with your preconceived idea about the truth and then morph the scriptures so they will fit into your pattern? It is not only a matter of integrity in handling the scriptures it is a matter of submission to the truth presented in the whole word of God. I guess the real question is this: when it comes to truth, which one has to change in order to fit, you or the Bible? The answer to that question has far reaching effects on your view of God, your doctrine, truth, and even your soul/spirit.

TRIBULATION PEOPLE

God is in control, even in what seems to be the worst possible circumstances. God always provides for a remnant, a group who is loyal to Him. With His love God continues to give chances for people to come to Him. And He willingly accepts all who do decide to accept Him into their life. Even though God allows governments to arise that persecute His people, these governments will eventually be destroyed. God does watch out for His own.

TRIBULATION EVENTS

Even in the midst of God's greatest display of anger against man and Satan, He still shows mercy in allowing people to come to Him. Studying these events should affect the way we view God. We must come to Him with respect and reverence, and not take His presence in our life lightly. We must gain a better sense of God's holiness, justice, and mercy, and seek those characteristics in our life.

RAPTURE

We must be ready. We must be accepters of Jesus and live lives that will prepare us for the judgment seat of Christ. Most importantly, we must understand that Jesus loves us immensely and intimately. He will come forcefully and with passion to retrieve us from this earth, to live with Him forever.

OVERALL

God did not have to share the future with us. He could have let it all be a big surprise. But, I believe He did share it so that we would have hope. As we struggle, feel sorrow and pain, in this life because of our sin, and the sin of others, we can have hope. We look forward to an eternity with Jesus, yet realizing that He is still here with us today. Jesus will never leave us or forsake us, now or in eternity. This is His promise, and our hope.

MIND THE GAP

As we have studied these future events we have seen two paths unfold. There are the accepters of God and what He has done for them, and then there are those who refuse God. The question for each person who walks this earth is, "Which path are you going to take?" My prayer is that each person reading this book will take the necessary steps to mind the gap between them and God, and then share that truth with others.

This thought is reflected in the closing chapter of the book of Revelation. Chapter 22, verse 17, tells us that the Spirit and the Bride (a reference to the church), invite people to come. God the Holy Spirit, working through those who are accepters, invites people to come into a relationship with Him. God offers life like a river of water. The water is cool and clear and refreshing. Whoever wishes to accept God into their life in order to mind the gap will receive the refreshment of life. There is nothing better. And you are invited to come.

APPENDIX

An Accepter's story

We all have it, especially me. It's that part of us that we just want to hide. We don't want it exposed during a job interview, or a date, or when we meet the new neighbors. It is the part of us that, when it moves to the surface and presents itself, causes negative consequences. The Bible term for this is sin. Anything that ultimately causes negative consequences is sin.

God is different than I am though. He is perfect. He is so full of goodness that evil and sin cannot penetrate Him. The Bible term for this is holy. God being perfect and me being, well, not, is one thing that causes a separation between us.

Sin   Absolute Good (Holy)
                                                                    GOD

Then, there is this thing called justice. That is what puts the huge gap between me and God. You see, justice demands that anyone who has ever committed even the smallest sin has to remain separated from God forever. It is a fact that, if I always listened to God and obeyed Him, I would never do anything that caused negative consequences. But, I don't always listen to Him. Instead, I rely on my own intelligence or moral compass to decide what is right or wrong. Occasionally, I will listen to someone else's definition of right, and end up doing something wrong. The point is, I am constantly creating negative consequences for myself and others because I am not listening to God.

Justice demands that, if I am not going to listen to God and obey Him, then I must remain separated from Him. If I don't want to listen to Him, then

I obviously don't want Him controlling my life. Therefore, the most just and fair thing to do is to allow me to remain separate from God so I don't have to listen to Him.

This separation is known as death. Physical death is caused when the soul/spirit separates from the physical body. And spiritual death is caused when the soul/spirit separates from God. That is the state I found myself in whenever I didn't listen to God. This state of being spiritually dead lasts forever, unless something changes.

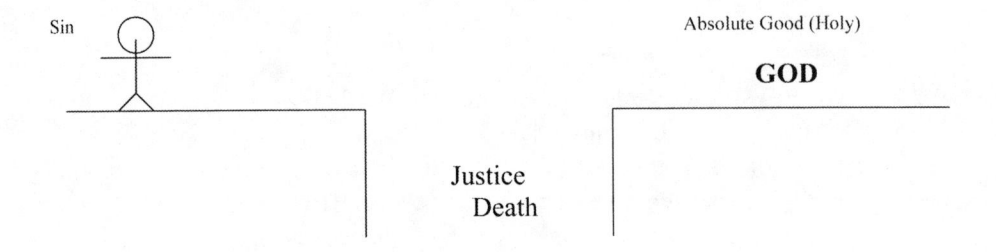

Sin   Absolute Good (Holy)
                                                                                                    GOD

                              Justice
                              Death

God is absolutely good, and He is full of love. But, this justice thing is something that He will not skirt around. He is a stickler for justice. So, now, God looks at me and sees that I am separated from Him because of the demands of justice. But, His love is demanding that I have a relationship with Him. After all, that is why He created me in the first place.

Interestingly enough, there is a loophole in justice. If one person could live a perfect life, always listen to God and obey Him, then that person would not deserve to die. He could live forever, and have a relationship with God forever. But, here's the loophole, if that person decided to give up his life, he would be able to pay the price of justice for everyone. He would die to satisfy the requirements of justice for everyone.

Unfortunately, no one could ever live the perfect life, completely following God. I definitely couldn't. So, God decided to become a man, and live as one of us; only, He was able to live a perfect life. Jesus came to earth and always did everything that God wanted Him to do. He did not cause any ultimate negative consequences for himself or others.

Jesus then gave up His life. He died so that God could give me mercy. When I do not receive the punishment I deserve, it is called mercy. Jesus died so that I would not have to receive the death sentence justice demanded. He put a stake through the heart of the death penalty justice demanded of me.

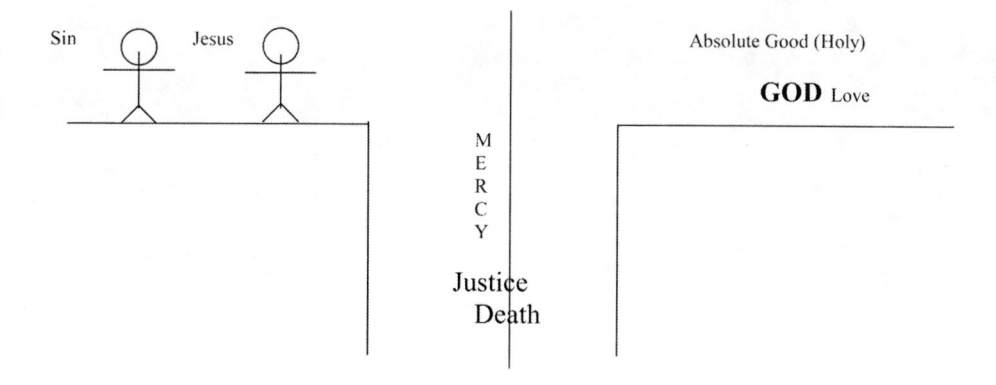

```
Sin    ○  Jesus  ○                          Absolute Good (Holy)
       ╱│╲      ╱│╲                              **GOD** Love
       ╱ ╲      ╱ ╲
_____                    _____
                        M
                        E
                        R
                        C
                        Y
                    Justice
                    Death
```

God could have stopped there. I could have received His mercy for me and lived forever. But that was not good enough for God. God wanted to give me something I did not deserve. This is called grace. God wanted to give me a relationship with Himself that would last forever. With grace, God fully bridged the gap between me and Him.

I asked Jesus to be a part of my life. It wasn't hard, just a simple prayer. "Jesus, I believe you died to pay the price of my sin so I would not have to. Please forgive me for the wrong that I have done, and be a part of my life. I want a relationship with you." Jesus died to give me mercy, and to have a relationship with me. But, He has never forced Himself on me. It was my decision to enter into a relationship with Him. Now, I have an everlasting relationship with God. I'm not perfect, but Jesus always stands up for me, and makes sure justice knows that He died for me to pay for my imperfection.

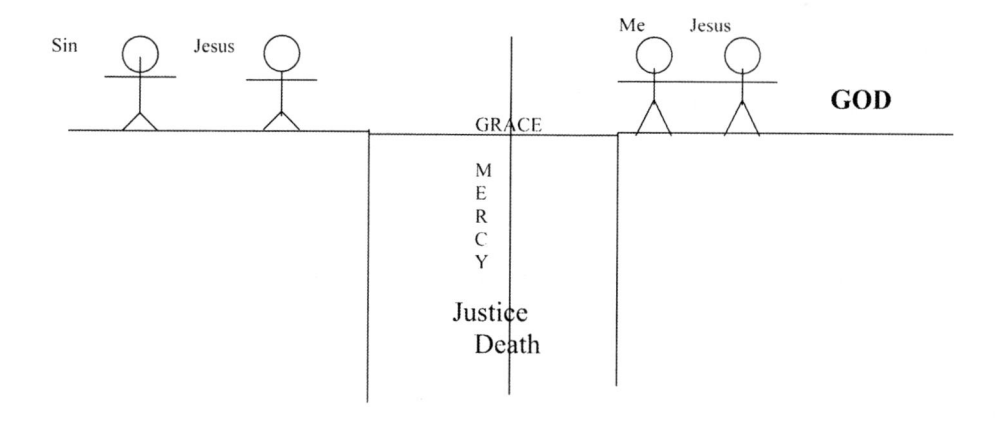

```
                                              Me    Jesus
Sin    ○  Jesus  ○                             ○     ○
       ╱│╲      ╱│╲                           ╱│╲   ╱│╲      **GOD**
_____  GRACE  _____
                        M
                        E
                        R
                        C
                        Y
                    Justice
                    Death
```

978-0-595-40370-7
0-595-40370-0